The Classical Tradition
in Operation

In these five essays Niall Rudd presents an eclectic set of comparisons between a number of ancient authors and later English writers ranging from Chaucer to Pound. He shows how five English authors consciously used and adapted classical works, and in so doing he illuminates both the classical authors and their English imitators and admirers. Readable translations and summaries of the Latin sources make these stimulating studies accessible even to scholars and students with little or no Latin.

The first essay compares Chaucer's treatment of Dido in *The House of Fame* and *The Legend of Good Women* with Virgil's presentation of Dido in the *Aeneid*, and Ovid's in *Heroides* 7. The second essay, comparing Shakespeare's *The Comedy of Errors* with Plautus' *Menaechmi*, demonstrates how Shakespeare, weaving Roman farce into the framework of Hellenistic romance, developed both genres into something richer and more complex. The third essay, on Pope's *Epistle to Augustus*, shows how he converted Horace's praise of Augustus into an anti-royalist attack on George II. In the fourth essay, Rudd discusses how much of Tennyson's *Lucretius* is invented and imported by Tennyson as a way of externalizing the inner conflicts he experienced in the age of doubt. The final essay, on Pound and Propertius, looks at Pound's representation of the Latin poet in *Homage to Sextus Propertius*, specifically in the areas of imperial politics, love, and language.

In his preface Rudd writes: 'Everyone knows of the Classical Tradition – comprehending it is another matter.' This book brings it closer to our understanding.

NIALL RUDD is Professor Emeritus, Department of Latin, Bristol University.

THE ROBSON CLASSICAL LECTURES

NIALL RUDD

The Classical Tradition in Operation

Chaucer / Virgil
Shakespeare / Plautus
Pope / Horace
Tennyson / Lucretius
Pound / Propertius

UNIVERSITY OF TORONTO PRESS
Toronto Buffalo London

Printed on acid-free paper

Canadian Cataloguing in Publication Data

Rudd, Niall
The classical tradition in operation

(The Robson classical lectures)
Includes bibliographical references and index.
Contents: Chaucer/Virgil – Shakespeare/Plautus –
Pope/Horace – Tennyson/Lucretius – Pound/Propertius.
ISBN 0-8020-0570-5

1. English poetry – History and criticism.
2. English poetry – Roman influences.
3. Literature, Comparative – English and Latin.
4. Literature, Comparative – Latin and English.
I. Title. II. Series.

PR508.C68R8 1994   821.009′142   C94-930658-4

This book has been published with
the help of a grant from Victoria University
in the University of Toronto.

To Ian and Jill

Contents

Foreword

This is the second volume of the Robson Classical Lectures to reach publication. The series takes its name from Donald Oakley Robson (1905–76), who graduated in Honours Classics from Victoria College in the University of Toronto in 1928. He went on to earn his MA (1929) and his PhD (1932) from the University of Toronto. After teaching at the University of Western Ontario for seventeen years, he returned to his *alma mater*, and taught Latin there from 1947 until his retirement in 1975. His wife, Rhena Victoria Kendrick (1901–82), also graduated in Honours Classics from Victoria College, in 1923, with the Governor General's Gold Medal. They were generous benefactors of their college. In Professor Robson's will, he made provision that, from time to time, several public lectures should be delivered on a classical theme by a distinguished scholar, and then, after appropriate revision, published.

The series will, we believe, have a wide appeal among those who are interested in ancient Greece and Rome, and in the culture of classical antiquity. We had the good fortune to persuade Niall Rudd, Professor Emeritus of Latin at the University of Bristol, to participate in our project. He had been our colleague at University College in the University of Toronto from 1959 to 1968. In November 1992 he returned to Toronto, and presented three public lectures on 'the classical tradition in operation.' They were greatly appreciated by his audience, which included both specialists and non-specialists; it was clear that they would provide the basis for a sound, scholarly, innovative book. We now present that book, a distinguished contribution to a distinguished series.

The Committee expresses its gratitude to the president of Victoria University, Eva Kushner, for her encouragement and support.

Wallace McLeod
for the Committee, 1993

MEMBERS OF THE COMMITTEE (1991–3)

J.M. Bigwood
A.M. Keith
W.E. McLeod, *Chairman*
K.R. Thompson
J.S. Traill
E.I. Robbins, *ex officio*

Preface

This book represents the third set of Robson Classical Lectures. In November 1992 three of the lectures were delivered in a shorter form in Victoria College, Toronto, the college to which Donald Oakley Robson devoted his professional career. The Committee's invitation to give them was especially welcome, since it allowed me to renew old friendships and to revive happy memories of the ten years which I spent on the staff of the university.

As for the subject, everyone knows of the Classical Tradition. Comprehending it is another matter. Gilbert Highet's encyclopaedic volume ignored such vast areas as thought, art, and law, confining itself to 'Greek and Roman Influences on Western Literature.' Even then, as its author acknowledged, its 800-odd pages provided no more than an outline. Other literary studies have concentrated on a country, or period, or genre, or writer. (The reader will readily supply examples.) Yet there remains a case for attempting something even narrower and more specific – a study which will focus on just two works at a time, showing in some detail how poets in different centuries have consciously used and adapted their Latin predecessors. Such a procedure calls for an apology. Only a polymath could claim to be familiar with all ten of the poets here under review. I am particularly aware of my amateur status in the area of English poetry. Nevertheless, if in our fragmented age there is to be any work of this kind, it has to be undertaken by one who is willing to rely on the indulgence of his professional colleagues.

I owe a heavy debt to the following fundamental works: the Riverside edition of Chaucer (J.M. Fyler, M.C.E. Shaner, and A.S.G. Edwards); the Arden edition of *The Comedy of Errors* (R.A. Foakes); the Twickenham edition of Pope (J. Butt); the Longman edition of Tennyson (C.B. Ricks); and *Ezra Pound and Sextus Propertius* (J.P. Sullivan). I should like to thank my former colleagues J.A. Burrow, G.P. Goold, D.W. Hopkins, A.J. Minnis, V.J. Scattergood, and T. Webb for help with various problems. I had the benefit of a conversation with Miss Margaret Hubbard on Propertius; Professor Elizabeth Asmis kindly provided material about Professor W.G. Hale; and two anonymous readers made constructive suggestions. The usual formula of absolution may be taken as read.

I should perhaps add that at one stage I had thought of trying to combine my exposition with some account of where I stood *vis-à-vis* recent critical theory. But it soon became clear that such an attempt would result in a less concrete and more polemical book. By eschewing the idiom of post-modernism (though not necessarily its concepts, of which not all are new) I am bound to offend certain schools of thought. But if you take the traditional view that every educated person is a citizen of the *respublica litterarum*, then it is better to be dubbed old-fashioned and simplistic than pretentious and esoteric.

N.R.

The Classical Tradition
in Operation

CHAPTER ONE

Chaucer and Virgil
Two Portraits of Dido

To speak of 'two portraits' is convenient shorthand for a more complex state of affairs. Chaucer presents Dido in two major passages – one in *The House of Fame* (*HF*), Book 1, the other in *The Legend of Good Women* (*LGW*), no. 3. And while his main source in each case is Virgil (Books 1 and 4 of the *Aeneid*), he does draw at certain points on the reduced and characteristically modified picture given by Ovid in his *Heroides*, no. 7. In this analysis we shall proceed chronologically, starting with the *Aeneid*.

To locate our discussion in the right area, we begin with a question: assuming there is a god, does he control history, or does he not? In his early, Epicurean, phase (if that is the correct tradition)[1] Virgil took the second view. The *Aeneid*, however, implies the first. It describes how, after the heroic age of Greece, power was transferred from Troy to Italy, where it eventually found its culmination and centre in Augustan Rome. No intermediate empires, even that of Alexander, are acknowledged, and no further transfers of power are envisaged. Roman rule will last for ever. From our vantage point such a conception of history seems selective, chauvinistic, and backward-looking; yet to an Italian of the first century BC it must have seemed natural enough. If god operated through history, then (allowing for disagreement over minor details) surely the rise of Rome was preordained. For how could such a momentous process have occurred without divine will? So the establishment of Trojan-Roman power in Italy, as described in the *Aeneid*, must reflect the plan of Jupiter or Fate.

For all we know, Virgil may have believed this (though it does not follow that he believed that the Romans were chosen for world dominion because of their superior moral qualities). But whatever his personal beliefs, one of his great achievements as an artist was to present those preordained events as the outcome of moral choices – choices which, however agonizing, were made by characters who believed they could have chosen otherwise. In Aeneas' own case, at three points in Book 2 he ignores divine instructions to leave Troy;[2] as late as Book 5, when the women have set fire to the boats in Sicily, he seriously considers abandoning the whole enterprise in despair;[3] in Book 4 he leaves Dido as a supreme act of will, not because his affections have faded,[4] but because his conscience has finally convinced him that he must fulfil a higher obligation.

While Virgil was not the first to bring Aeneas to Carthage, it seems most likely that he was the first to present Dido and Aeneas as lovers.[5] How, then, did he mean us to judge the affair and its outcome? Those who believe that the *Aeneid* was written to celebrate the victory of light over darkness find several reasons for treating Dido with suspicion. As founder of Carthage, she was identified with Rome's inveterate enemy – a people notorious for treachery and barbarism; and she revealed her savage nature in a curse which foretold the horrors of the Punic wars (4.607–31). On a personal level, by accepting Aeneas as a lover, she broke her oath to remain a widow or *uniuira* (4.241–7), and neglected her duty to her subjects. For some or all of these reasons Dido, in antiquity and in modern times, has been judged weak or even vicious. A few scholars have even had the moral self-assurance to proclaim that her death was deserved.[6]

Now if Virgil really intended us to regard Dido as sinister or immoral or even (more sympathetically) as the embodiment of an outmoded heroism (i.e., a selfish desire for glory), he could have saved his readers a lot of trouble by saying so. A word or two in Book 1, slipped into Venus' introductory speech, would have put us wise; or in Book 7, in the prelude to the war against Turnus, Virgil could easily have said that he was about to sing of the triumph of *pietas* over *furor*, or something equally edifying. But he never did. Instead, while presenting Dido as the enemy of

Rome-to-be, he took pains to describe her as queenly, noble, and generous. (Before she has even met Aeneas, she offers the Trojan refugees a place in her kingdom.)[7] Perhaps he had learned from Homer that an enemy can be hostile without being inferior, and that if you portray the vanquished as unworthy you diminish the glory of the victor. At any rate the description of Dido in Book 1 is remarkably free from that atavistic hatred which seems to have lingered in the memory of so many of Virgil's contemporaries, even though the Punic menace had ceased with the destruction of Carthage over 120 years before, and new settlements had been planted there by Julius Caesar and Octavian.[8]

As for Dido's curse (4.615ff.), that was uttered in a frenzy of rage and humiliation. She was, after all, a queen. Think of the scorn that would have been heaped upon Virgil had he shown her waving a brave farewell to her departing lover, and then retiring to shed a tear in the privacy of her boudoir. As for remaining a widow, there is no evidence that this would have been expected by contemporary Romans, and some evidence to the contrary.[9] In accepting Aeneas as a lover (which she did, remember, with the combined approval of Venus and Juno) she apparently deceived herself into believing he had become her husband; but the charge of neglecting her people comes only from *Fama* (4.194), a filthy goddess who deals in truth and falsehood alike (4.188, 195). In other words while it was strictly true that Aeneas was *regni immemor* (4.225, 267), the same was, at the most, temporarily true of Dido. (The building operations which have broken off in 4.86–9 have been resumed by 260.) Proof that the liaison was *not* contrary to the interests of Carthage is provided by the fact that Juno, who presided over Carthage and was most committed to its welfare, was keen for Aeneas to stay. On a human level the arguments in favour of the attachment are cogently presented by Anna: the queen wanted love and affection; both she and Carthage needed royal children; and all required security if the city were to achieve future glory (4.30–53).

Those who censure Dido are equally critical of Juno.[10] But the same points apply. Juno had *her* plan for world history, whereby Carthage was to be the great world power. There was nothing intrinsically evil in that; it just happened not to be the plan of

Jupiter and the Fates. True, Juno had *heard* that the Fates intended otherwise (1.22); but her pride would not have allowed her to make further inquiries. When she exclaims *quippe uetor fatis!* (1.39), she does so, as Austin says, with indignant irony. The great goddess is certainly not going to withdraw without a fight; if need be, she can literally raise hell:

> flectere si nequeo superos, Acheronta mouebo. (7.312)

In the end, at long last, she does withdraw, as Jupiter foretells (1.279–82); but on what terms? The Latins, she stipulates, are to retain their name, their language, and their national dress; Troy is to remain forever fallen (12.823–8). Jupiter smilingly assents, and promises for good measure that the Latins will retain their customs; he himself will add certain religious rites. Apart from Aeneas' all-important contribution to the royal blood, the Trojans are to 'sink down in the mass' (12.835–6). These unfavourable terms were foreshadowed in Dido's curse: *leges pacis iniquae* (4.618); but they were certainly never imagined by the Trojans themselves as they struggled across to Italy from the ruins of Ilium. Yet for Virgil that was necessity. To put it in non-theological terms, the Romans lived in Latium and spoke Latin; they did not observe Trojan customs or wear Trojan dress. So Virgil *had* to point his epic towards a Latin future. And whatever his personal beliefs may have been, as a poet writing in the Homeric tradition, he had to represent the events of his story as reflecting the manoeuvres of the gods.

Such, then, is the majestic stage on which Virgil's Dido performs. While conservative, patriotic, Roman men may well have thought of her as a dangerous temptress or as a symbol of ancient enmity,[11] others remembered her sympathetically as a star-crossed lover. When Ovid says that no part of the *Aeneid* is more popular than 'love united by an illicit compact' (*Tristia* 2.535–6), he is not talking about the foreshadowing of the Punic wars. When the educated woman, whom Juvenal in the second century finds so unappealing, takes Dido's part, 'forgiving the doomed Elissa' (6.435), she is presented as a type; there are lots more like her. And when Macrobius in the fourth century observes how the story of the wanton Dido (*fabula lasciuientis Didonis*) has been made the subject of paintings, statues, tapestries, plays, and songs (*Saturnalia* 5.17.5), he is paying tribute to the power of a great imaginative artist over the human heart (*quod pectoribus humanis dulcedo fingentis infudit*) – a power which was so memorably felt by the young Augustine (*Confessions* 1.13). All this suggests that in Roman, as in modern, times not everyone condemned Dido; that then, as now, the pharisees did not have it all their own way.

When Ovid read Book 4 of the *Aeneid*, he will have noted the following features: (1) Virgil's explanation of Aeneas' departure as an act of obedience to the will of god; (2) Dido's interpretation of his departure as an act of callous treachery; and (3) Virgil's presentation of Dido not only as a noble and dynamic queen, but also as a woman in love, a woman who is successively passionate, reproachful, pathetic, vengeful, abject, despairing, cursing, and finally resigned. In regard to (1), large questions about the rise of Rome and the course of history were quite irrelevant to the *Heroides* – a collection of letters supposedly written by women to their former lovers.[12] Such questions seem, indeed, never to have engaged Ovid's interest. It is significant that later, when he came to retrace the wanderings of Aeneas in his own great quasi-epic (*Metamorphoses* 13 and 14), he should have used the hero's journeys mainly as a line on which to hang a series of richly embroidered stories. There, too, despite the chronological framework, the philosophy of world history was a dimension which did not concern him; nor was he interested in the moral dilemma of Aeneas.

In regard to (2), as the seventh epistle purports to be written by Dido, without any editorial comment on Ovid's part, it naturally provides only her interpretation of Aeneas' behaviour. In this important respect, Ovid's Dido is the same as Virgil's. In the *Aeneid* the queen failed to hear, or rather failed to take in, the prophecies about the Trojans' future which Aeneas reported in his narrative (2.781ff.; 3.163ff.; 253ff.; 377ff.). When, later, he tells her about his guilty dreams of Anchises (4.351–5) and his vision of Mercury (4.356–9), she thrusts it all impatiently aside – as if the gods above bothered about such matters (4.379–80)! All she can see is that after accepting her love and protection for a considerable time, during which he kept discreetly quiet about his higher mission, Aeneas is now suddenly and inexplicably on the point of leaving. She can hardly be blamed if she castigates him for treachery – *perfide* (305, 366), *perfidus ille* (421). Similarly Ovid's Dido has no conception of why Aeneas is leaving her. Clearly his decision is not based on any idea of self-interest – he does not know where Italy is (10); he cannot expect to be made a present of any new territory (15–16); nor can he hope to find a wife who will love him as she does (22); if he reaches the Tiber he will be a total stranger (146). Yes, she has heard about his gods. But if he is really under their protection, why has he been driven across the sea for seven years (87)? She has also heard about Mercury's orders – *sed iubet ire deus* (139). But instead of trying to understand the meaning of 'a god bids you go,' she turns it into a rather feeble debating point: 'I wish he had forbidden you to come.' The only conclusion she can reach is that Aeneas has been false from the beginning. As Virgil's Dido said, his behaviour has been all treachery – *perfidiae* (58), *perfide* (79). In the *Fasti*, however, the few lines given to Aeneas show him in a sympathetic light (3.612ff.). His words, reminiscent of those spoken in *Aeneid* 6.455ff., are *not* those of a traitor; and the context carries no allegations of insincerity.

In regard to (3) – i.e., the character of Virgil's Dido and her changing moods -we must bear in mind the form in which Ovid was working. The *Epistle* is written at a single moment of Dido's life. Therefore, although it allows her to reminisce about her past and to move from one kind of appeal to another, it cannot begin to rival the scope of Virgil's account, which unfolds over a period of time, describing the events in vivid narrative and also dramatizing them in a succession of scenes both on earth and in heaven. The *Epistle*'s form is related to its emotional effect. Since Ovid's prime concern is to convey an impression of reproachful pathos, this involves a notable reduction in Dido's stature as a heroine. Granted, Ovid acknowledges she is a queen – specifically in the compressed account of her escape from Troy and her arrival in Carthage. But because he is presenting her as above all an object of sympathy, he portrays her in the main as a passive victim of fate, driven into exile, pursued by enemies, threatened by neighbouring kingdoms, beleaguered by suitors (111–24). The corresponding passage in Virgil begins *imperium Dido Tyria regit urbe profecta* (1.340), 'Dido wields authority here, having come from the city of Tyre.' The escape from Tyre ends with the sentence *dux femina facti* (1.364), 'a woman was the leader of the enterprise.' At the end of the whole tragic story, when she has recovered her poise, Virgil's queen surveys her achievements:

> uixi, et quem dederat cursum Fortuna peregi,
> et nunc magna mei sub terras ibit imago.
> urbem praeclaram statui, mea moenia uidi (4.653–5)

> I have lived, and I have completed the course which Fortune assigned, and now a great ghost of me will go down below the earth. I have founded a splendid city, I have seen my own walls.

Such magnificence is quite beyond the range of Ovid's *Epistle*.

As he has diminished her regal nobility, so he has damped down her ferocity. Virgil's Dido, inflamed with fury, hurls back Aeneas' phrase (*Italiam non sponte sequor*) in his teeth: *i, sequere Italiam uentis* (381), 'Go, make for Italy with the winds!,' invoking an improbable shipwreck: 'I hope that on the rocks in mid ocean you will gulp down your punishment, calling again and again on the name of Dido.' In Ovid's *Epistle* Dido is altogether gentler. She hopes Aeneas will *not* be shipwrecked and drink the seawater, but rather survive with the reputation of having caused her death (62ff.). If he does drown (and she hopes he won't), he will see the image of the woman he has deceived and will know that the gods have aimed their bolts at *him* (65ff.). Needless to say, this lady could not conceive, much less utter, the terrible curses hurled by her predecessor at Aeneas and all his descendants (*Aeneid* 4.615–29).

What Ovid has done, then, is to focus on the pathos of Virgil's Dido, as shown in *Aeneid* 4.314–30 and 408–36, producing what might be called a reduction with variations. The main types of variation involve inverting or extending Virgilian motifs. We have already noted one example of inversion. Virgil's Dido says 'may

you drown'; Ovid's says 'may you *not* drown.' In the *Aeneid*,
Mercury says Aeneas must leave for the sake of Ascanius (4.274f.,
cf. 234); in the *Epistle*, Dido says 'at least *postpone* leaving for
the sake of Ascanius' (75–8). In his final ultimatum Mercury says
'No more delay.' *uarium et mutabile semper / femina* (4.569–70)
– i.e., she may become aggressive and send soldiers to prevent
your departure.[13] The Ovidian Dido says 'I only wish you were as
changeable (*mutabilis*) as the winds, for they will eventually
become gentle and friendly' (51). By 'extension' I mean the habit
of taking a Virgilian expression or idea and pushing it one stage
further. In the *Aeneid*, Dido cries 'So this is the good faith of the
man who, they say (*aiunt*), carries his ancestral gods with him,
who bore on his shoulders his aged father' (4.597–9). Ovid seized
on the hint of scepticism in *aiunt* and pushed it into an accusa-
tion of mendacity: 'You do *not* carry your gods with you; nor, as
you boast, you traitor, did the sacred relics or your father ever
rest on your shoulders. Those are all lies!' (79–81). In the *Aeneid*,
in the darkness and confusion of the sack of Troy, Creusa somehow becomes separated from the party (2.738–40). In the *Epistle*,
according to Dido, Creusa was simply abandoned by her callous
husband (84). Whereas Virgil's queen sadly points out that if
Aeneas leaves she will have no little son to remind her of him
(4.327–30), Ovid's Dido claims that she may be pregnant (133).
One more example may be added, for it will prepare for our next
point. In Virgil, Dido asks, 'Are you putting to sea even in such
wintry weather?' (4.309). In Ovid, after giving a similar warning,
she adds, '[The sea is dangerous to the faithless, especially when
they have done an injury to love]; for it was from the waters of
Cythera that the mother of the Loves is said to have risen naked'
(56–60). Ovid seems to have started from the topos so well expressed by Sedley: 'Love still has something of the Sea, / From
whence his mother rose.' He has then extended and varied the
idea, so as to claim that, if Love is wounded, the sea (in virtue of
its association with Venus) will punish the wrong-doer. This is
not only odd, in that it ascribes to Venus a constant concern for
justice; it is here quite absurd, in that the wrong-doer is Venus'
own son. One suspects that Ovid cannot resist that picturesque
Hellenistic *exemplum*, with its inevitable nudity, even though

such an image is totally inappropriate to the dramatic context and would not, in any case, have occurred to a woman in Dido's state of mind.

This brings us to Ovid's rhetoric. There is nothing wrong with rhetoric *per se*; it is simply the persuasive use of language. But what if, instead of lending persuasiveness to a character's case, it calls attention to the writer's ingenuity? In Ovid's *Epistle*, after the image of the dying swan, which is effective enough, we are immediately surprised by a wearily sardonic phrase: 'I'm not writing to you because I hope to change your mind [this nullifies at the outset the *Epistle*'s whole *raison d'être*]; but since I have utterly wasted my kind deeds, my reputation, and my modesty of body and soul, it is of little consequence to waste words' (3–6). Then comes a zeugma: 'Are the same winds to carry away your sails and your promises?' (8). This is immediately repeated with a variation: 'Are you determined to cast off your pledge along with your ship?' (9). Later we are treated to some clever grammatical manoeuvres in chiastic form:

perdita ne perdam, timeo, noceamue nocenti (61)

Ruined as I am, I am afraid to ruin or harm one who harms me.

The neatness of the line will be appreciated by anyone who tries to translate it. It recalls some of the delightful word-play in the *Amores* and *Ars Amatoria*; but how appropriate is such a line to a woman on the point of suicide?

We are talking of appropriateness rather than realism. Nothing, after all, could be less realistic than the highly wrought declamation delivered by Ariadne, in disarray, in the surf of Naxos, beginning

sicine me patriis auectam, perfide, ab aris,
perfide, deserto liquisti in litore, Theseu? (Catullus 64.132–3)

Is it thus that after luring me away from my family's altars, you traitor, you have left me, you traitor, on this deserted shore, Theseus?

This, of course, is rhetoric. It is as if Catullus were determined to give his Ariadne all the best arguments and the most effective phrases to secure a conviction from an unseen jury. Clearly many Romans found such emotional appeals effective – we need only think of the brilliant career of Cicero. In literature the line of wronged and eloquent women stretched back from Virgil's Dido, through Catullus' Ariadne, to Medea and other heroines of tragedy (Roman and Greek). Their rhetoric was accepted as long as it seemed appropriate to their character and situation. (That was one of Horace's points in the *Ars Poetica*.)[14] For writer and reader it was all a matter of taste and judgment. But already in antiquity there were reservations about Ovid's judgment, as we know from the two Senecas and Quintilian.[15] Such misgivings were given their classic expression by Dryden;[16] and they reappear in the books of Wilkinson and Jacobson in our own time.[17]

In the last thirty years or so some defenders have come forward. Professor Winsor Leach, whose thesis I have heard of only indirectly,[18] maintained that the *Heroides* were *mock*-declamations, full of deliberate absurdities. Granted, some of the passages do come close to absurdity. (One recalls Ronald Knox's mischievous epistle written to Penelope by Odysseus from inside the Trojan horse.)[19] But the idea would be more persuasive if there had been a large body of heroic epistles written by others; then Ovid's might be taken as parody. Also the witty strokes of language do not seem to be quite frequent enough to support the theory; even Ovid, who did not know when to leave well enough alone, would hardly have prolonged the joke for more than twenty epistles. Professor Anderson argues that Ovid has presented a charming, sophisticated Dido, who is clever enough to produce witty phrases.[20] The difficulty here is to imagine simple pathos blended in the same personality with that kind of playful dexterity. Most readers have the impression that while the tears are Dido's tears, the wit is the wit of Ovid. More recently, Dr Hopkins has cast his net more widely, discussing the whole matter of 'Dryden and Ovid's "wit out of season".'[21] He speaks of 'Ovid's refusal to align himself,' of 'a distance which enables us to see [his characters'] conduct and thoughts in many different lights' (189). This interesting idea deserves more discussion than I can give it here, as indeed do the other two; but even if it is true that, say, the battle of the Lapiths and Centaurs (*Metamorphoses* 12.210ff.) can be seen simultaneously from both a clinically objective standpoint (with accurate pictures of mutilation) and a sympathetically subjective standpoint (with a vivid realization of rage and fear), I am not sure that the same holds good of a piece like *Heroides* 7, where the narrator is also the sufferer. It is perhaps worth remarking that although the *Metamorphoses* contains two dozen or more speeches made by grievously distressed women, none displays the same degree of verbal ingenuity that we find in Dido's letter. It probably has to be admitted that like other very witty people Ovid was not always prudent or discreet. (One thinks of Oscar Wilde sabotaging his own case at the Queensbury trial.) Even very late, in his exile poetry, the occasional jab of satire must have spoiled the picture of a penitent subject who sincerely admired his sovereign.

Returning, then, to *Heroides* 7, what has Ovid given us? Not a new, independent creation; for the *Epistle* presupposes the *Aeneid* and alludes to it throughout. Is it then a 'subversion' of Virgil's portrait? Hardly that either; for, as we have observed, Virgil's queen is, in two major scenes, intensely pathetic; she is also convinced that Aeneas is no more than a treacherous rat. More generally, 'subversion,' with its connotations of hostility, does not describe how Ovid is treating Virgil. He certainly has no intention of overturning or overthrowing his predecessor. What we have is, rather (as already argued), a reduction in scope, combined with a concentration on certain details. Ignoring the whole context of the epic, with its intimations of Rome's destiny, and leaving out Dido's nobility and ferocity, Ovid zooms in to focus on the thoughts and feelings of an aggrieved woman, whose desertion is the central fact that we are asked to consider. In its manipulation of language and metre the *Epistle* is a highly accomplished piece of writing; but its cleverness and pathos do not produce a satisfactory blend. In making this judgment we will avoid unfairness if we remember that we are comparing a relatively early epistle of Ovid with the greatest episode in Virgil's greatest poem. Ovid's own major, and distinctive, achievement lay twenty years ahead.

Nearly fourteen centuries separated Chaucer from Virgil and Ovid. He almost certainly did not know their works *in toto;* and there is evidence that at least some of what he did know was read with the aid of translations.[22] Moreover, one cannot go far in the scholarly literature before becoming aware of his debt (not necessarily more direct or immediate) to a range of medieval poetry in French and Italian.[23] Nevertheless, in his early work at least, the classical links were there; and in the case of *Aeneid* 1 and 4 and *Heroides* 7 it is widely accepted that he had the Latin at hand. So at the end of the twentieth century there may be some value (if only a novelty value) in approaching the two relevant works from that direction.

The opening of *The House of Fame* shows that Chaucer is *au fait* with various theories about dreams;[24] but he does not commit himself to any of them, and this agnostic stance is worth keeping in mind when we try to assess his mood at the conclusion of the poem. After invoking the god of sleep, the narrator proceeds to recount a dream in which he finds himself at first in the temple of Venus. The building is made of glass – a fragile and deceptive material – and it contains a picture of the goddess. Then come scenes from the *Aeneid*, naturally enough, because Aeneas was Venus' son. At three points in a very abridged account of Books 1 and 2 we are shown the goddess presiding over the course of Aeneas' life: first, she urges him to escape from Troy (162–5); then she begs Jupiter to save the Trojans from Juno's storm (213–18);[25] and finally she comforts Aeneas and sends him on his way to Carthage (235–8). After the stay in Carthage and the much briefer interlude in Sicily, Chaucer tells of a stormy crossing to Italy.[26] He mentions the visit to Hades, the arrival in Latium, and the war against Turnus. Although he omits some crucial interventions on the part of Venus (how she obtained armour from Vulcan, appeared on the battlefield, and healed her son's wound), he does report how

> mawgree Juno, Eneas,   (in spite of)
> For al hir sleight and hir compas,   (cunning)
> Acheved al his aventure,

For Jupiter took of hym cure   (care)
At the prayer of Venus. (461–5)

What, we may ask, is the *Aeneid* doing in a poem about fame? Perhaps the shortest answer is that, as Dante's *Divine Comedy* is often seen as a kind of *summa* of medieval thought, so a similar case could be made for the *Aeneid* in regard to classical antiquity. Virgil's epic conveys multifarious and influential testimony about the Graeco-Roman world, and hence about the experience of the West. Since this testimony is made up of fiction and speculation as well as fact, it cannot be classified simply as 'history.' Yet, along with the poem in which it is embodied, it can be brought under the general heading of 'what is said.' And that, in its broadest and most basic sense (from *for, fari*, 'I say'), is what 'fame' means here.

Now at several points in the *Aeneid* Venus appears as a loving mother, anxious for her son's safety and ambitious for his future. But at Carthage, along with this, we see quite a different side of her character. In spite of Jupiter's prophecy about Trojan Rome's future greatness (1.257–96), Venus is still not reassured. Juno, she knows, is determined to prevent Aeneas from reaching Italy. So to forestall any threat which Juno might cause through Dido's Carthaginians, Venus makes the queen fall passionately in love with Aeneas. Juno, for her own quite opposite reasons, collaborates. This unappealing manoeuvre, in which Venus reveals the erotic side of her divine personality, results in a disastrous mess. This can be seen in the fact that when it comes to getting Aeneas *out* of Carthage she has no part to play. The son whom she was so anxious to protect suffers one of his most agonizing experiences; and poor Dido, after being used by both goddesses, is discarded by Venus and failed by Juno. So when, after reading the *Aeneid*, we move on to *The House of Fame*, one conclusion to be drawn is that the goddess whose picture dominates her glassy temple is not to be trusted.

However that may be, it is also clear that the love affair which Venus instigated was, for Chaucer, by far the most interesting episode in Virgil's poem. In *The House of Fame* he gives it a central position; and, after recounting the story once, he then abandons narrative and lets Dido speak in her own words. As we are concerned with the classical tradition, it is worth pausing at this point. In his narrative of the affair (257–95) Chaucer makes some down-to-earth observations on the risks of falling for a stranger. The risks come from male unreliability:

> som man, of his pure kynde,   (essential nature)
> Wol shewen outward the fayreste,
> Tyl he have caught that what him leste. (280–2)
>
>   (pleases him)

This particular formulation is not uttered by Virgil's or Ovid's Dido, or by any of Ovid's heroines. It does occur in the lament of Catullus' Ariadne:

> nunc iam nulla uiro iuranti femina credat,
> nulla uiri speret sermones esse fideles;
> quis dum aliquid cupiens animus praegestit apisci,
> nil metuunt iurare, nihil promittere parcunt (64.143–6)

> From now on let no woman believe a man's oaths, nor expect that a man's speeches are reliable. While their lustful mind is eager to obtain something, they do not scruple to swear anything; they are unsparing with their promises.

And the first line of this is quoted by Ovid's Ariadne (*Fasti*, 3.475). Nevertheless, Chaucer's comment may be quite independent. In 314, he claims to be drawing only on his own dream: 'Non other auctour alegge I.' Certainly one would not want to deny what Jill Mann (1991) calls his 'act of imaginative retrieval' (15).

The same general topic recurs in Dido's bitter question: 'Allas, is every man thus trewe?' (301), and again in 332ff.:

> Allas, that ever hadde routhe
> Any woman on any man! ...
> How sore that ye men konne groone,

Anoon as we have yow receyved,
Certaynly we ben deceyved!

Later on (388ff.) male deceit is illustrated by the examples of
Demophon, Achilles, Paris, Jason, Hercules, and Theseus – all of
whom occur, in that sequence,[27] in the *Heroides*. So it is fair to
argue that, to reinforce his general idea about men, Chaucer has
drawn on the *Heroides* – as a *collection*. That does not mean,
however, that he is drawing on either Virgil's or Ovid's Dido. A
further indication of Chaucer's independence in this section is
that in lines 287–8 he says that, for all Aeneas' treachery, Dido
was not blameless; he speaks of 'hir nyce lest,' her foolish desire,[28] which led her to love too soon a guest whom she hardly
knew. It is notable that while Virgil refers several times to Dido's
madness, he never speaks of folly – another reason why one
should not be too quick to allot blame.

After ending his account in 374, Chaucer says (in paraphrase)
'if you want to know how the queen died and what she said, read
the *Aeneid* [i.e., 4.504–8, 642–62]; if you want to know what she
wrote before her death, read Ovid's *Epistle*. If the *Epistle* were not
too long, I'd write it out.' This indicates quite correctly that, as
far as content is concerned, those forty-odd lines of the *Aeneid*
and the whole of Ovid's *Epistle* contributed almost nothing to the
composition of *The House of Fame*.

So much for Chaucer's narrative. What about the speech which
he gives to Dido?

'Allas!' quod she, 'my swete herte,
Have pitee on my sorwes smerte,
And slee mee not! Goo noght awey!
O woful Dido, wel-away!' (315–18)

These, and the lines which follow, are emotionally and poetically
the high point of the book. How is the speech related to the
tradition? 'Her complaint in Chaucer's version is much more like
that of Ovid's *Epistle*. She bemoans her disgrace as in Ovid; the
prevailing note is one of woe and distress, not of wrath as in the
Aeneid' (59). That is E.F. Shannon, writing in 1929.[29] The same

scholar adds 'It was the emphasis upon the fickleness of Aeneas and the disgrace of Dido that he got from Ovid' (76). In a matter of this kind there is no need to accept Shannon, or anyone else, as 'a man of gret auctorite.' One has only to consult *Heroides* 7 and the relevant passages of *Aeneid* 4.

It is true that in the *Epistle* (5–6) Dido regrets the loss of her *fama* along with her chastity, and that again in 97–8 she speaks of her *laesus pudor* ('injured modesty'). But in these respects she is no different from her Virgilian predecessor, who laments her *exstinctus pudor* and her *fama prior* (4.322–3). Chaucer's Dido says nothing about her chastity as such; she is primarily concerned with her reputation and what people are saying about her:

> O wel-awey that I was born!
> For thorgh yow is my name lorn,   (lost)
> And alle myn actes red and songe
> Over al thys lond on every tonge. (345–8)

She then goes on to quote the kind of thing that is being muttered (358–60) – cf. the half-true gossip in *Aeneid*.4.193–5; all the malicious talk, she says, is due to 'wikke Fame' – swift, omniscient, and misty (349–52). This description is obviously based on Virgil's *Fama*, which is swift (4.174–5, 180) and covered in clouds (177). That figure does not appear in Ovid. As for woe and distress, there is plenty of both in the *Aeneid* too, and there is no lack of emphasis on Aeneas' fickleness. The crucial distinction here is that, when Virgil's Dido explains Aeneas' behaviour in terms of fickleness, the reader knows she is wrong. Ovid's reader is given no information either way. But Chaucer's is told she is right:

> For he to hir a traytour was (267)
> ...
> How he betrayed hir, allas,
> And lefte hir ful unkyndely. (294–5)

These lines quite obliterate the passing references to Aeneas' destiny in 145 and 187–8. Nevertheless, the different perspective which results is a difference in the *narrator's* and the *reader's* perspective, not in that of Dido.

One further parallel, of a rhetorical sort, shows that (perhaps quite unconsciously) Chaucer has Virgil in mind. In *Aeneid* 4.307–8 Dido pleads:

> nec te noster amor nec te data dextera quondam
> nec moritura tenet crudeli funere Dido?

> Does not our love hold you back, nor the pledge once given by our right hands, nor the cruel death which Dido is going to die?

In *HF* 321–4 she says

> O that your love, ne your bond
> That ye have sworn with your ryght hond,
> Ne my crewel deth, quod she,
> May holde yow stille here with me!

There is no such correspondence in the *Epistle*.

There remains the undoubted fact that Chaucer's Dido, like Ovid's, is neither regal nor formidable. Yet even here a distinction has to be observed – a stylistic distinction. In Chaucer, Dido is moving because he allows her to speak simply. As Bennett says, 'his taste would not [perhaps could not] admit the conceits and epigrams which destroy any sense that Ovid's Dido is heartbroken' (1968, 36). It is this simplicity of language, neither Virgilian nor Ovidian, that establishes Chaucer's independence.

Before we leave Book 1 there is one surprise in store. When the episode is over and Aeneas is about to leave, Chaucer adds as a kind of afterthought:

> But to excusen Eneas
> Fullyche of al his grete trespas,
> The book seyth Mercurie, sauns fayle,
> Bad hym goo into Itayle,
> And leve Auffrikes regioun,

And Dido and hir faire toun. (427–32)[30]

No attempt is made to reconcile this passage with those that have gone before. They are simply allowed to stand in contradiction – perhaps yet another sign that human testimony is often conflicting.[31]

The next two books must be summarized very briefly to show how the story from the *Aeneid* fits into the scheme of the poem as a whole. On emerging from the temple of Venus, the poet finds himself in a desert place.[32] The vision, for all its wonder, was no more than 'fantome and illusion,' and brought no sure tidings about love. Emotionally and intellectually he has lost his bearings. At this point the eagle of Jupiter appears and snatches him aloft. It explains it has instructions to carry him to the house of Fame, where (in return for his devoted service to Cupid and Venus) he will hear

> Mo wonder thynges ...   (more)
> And of Loves folk moo tydynges,
> Both sothe sawes and lesinges (674–6)   (true sayings and lies)

This information, in some way a continuation of that provided in Book 1, will bring enlightenment and profit (579), and also sport and entertainment (664, 671, 886). In the meantime much instruction is provided *en route* by the eagle, which has had an extensive education and refers effortlessly to Greek philosophy, Greek myth, and such authorities on flight as Alexander and Scipio.[33] It also delivers a technical disquisition on sound, explaining how it is produced and how it reaches the house of Fame. The poet, meanwhile, hangs there, a naïve and astonished listener. There is perhaps a danger, however, that in this book we may concentrate too exclusively on the eagle. For all his knowledge and volubility, he is little more than an aerial taxi man. His boss is the same Jupiter who presided over the events portrayed in the temple of Venus. As there he took care of Venus' son, here he is giving a treat to Venus' poet by awarding him a flight in space, combined with a lecture on Western culture. The change from Book 1 is not so much a break in the subject of the narrative as an alteration of tone.

For his description of the house of Fame Chaucer takes a few hints from what Ovid says in *Metamorphoses* 12.39ff.[34] There is one significant difference. Whereas Ovid's house is made of re-sounding brass, Chaucer's is not. First, it stands on a rock 'of yse and not of stel' (1130). The feature, derived from a French poem on the house of Fortune, was doubtless chosen because it made the ascent slippery. But the result was to establish a link with the glass temple of Venus; for we are told that the rock was like crystallized alum, which is called 'alum de glas' (1124). Moreover, the building had 'walles of berile / That shoone ful lyghter than a glas' (1288–9).[35] Not surprisingly, details of both buildings are elaborated in terms which can be paralleled from fourteenth-century decoration.[36]

Situated between heaven and earth, the house of Fame receives everything that is said, including, by extension, everything that is said in the arts. Inside, on a high throne, sits Fame herself (1360ff.). Here we have the strongest link with Book 1, for Fame turns out to be a Chaucerian expansion of Virgil's monster (*Aeneid* 4.176ff.). It will be recalled that, in the story of Dido and Aeneas, *Fama* played a cardinal role by turning delight into disaster. For it was thanks to her that Jupiter's attention was drawn to the deepening involvement of Aeneas. Here, now, is Fame at home, in all her glory, dispensing renown and obscurity. Her method, which closely resembles that of her sister Fortune, turns out to be a non-method, for it is based entirely on caprice. She listens to prayers from nine groups of people and makes decisions which have no moral, indeed no rational, justification; some in fact are contradictory. Understandably baffled, the poet says in effect, 'I was told I would hear news of all kinds, in particular about love; but this isn't it' (1894–5). A bystander says, 'I know what you want to hear. Come with me' (1910–15). They proceed to a building near by.

To call this place 'the house of Rumour,' as many scholars do, is misleading. Chaucer does not call it that; and after the house of Fame such a name would imply a parallel figure, who presided over all the tittle-tattle. In fact there is no such figure. The place is a sort of vast annexe of the house of Fame (Under the castel, faste by). Its very close connection with the castle can also be seen in its conception. In creating it, Chaucer has taken certain features from Ovid's house of Fame, e.g., the ever-open doors (1951–3), the lack of rest (1956), the whispers (1958, 2044), and the crowds (2034). While the labyrinthine house is, indeed, the centre of rumour, everything said there eventually finds its way to Fame (2110–11). She classifies each item, and determines its duration (2112–17). Thus rumour is really one aspect or function of Fame.

Soon after they reach the super-labyrinth, the eagle reappears and secures entry to the building, which is a revolving structure sixty miles long, made out of twigs. Huge crowds mill about whispering. At length the poet moves over to a corner where people are exchanging reports about love (2142–3). In all the confusion he notices one who

semed for to be
A man of gret auctorite. (2157–8)

He, surely, will explain everything. But at this point the poem breaks off.

Or does it? There is much debate as to whether the present ending is as Chaucer intended. Various opinions are summarized in the Riverside edition (990), and also by Benson (1984) and Burrow (1991). If we had solid evidence of a different ending (whether planned and then abandoned, or written and subsequently lost) – an ending consisting of some kind of super-natural revelation, after which the poet awakes – then our inter-pretation of the work would have to be modified. But with the ending as it is, the vision can hardly fail to seem sceptical or at least agnostic. (One recalls Chaucer's non-committal attitude to dream theories at the beginning.) Whether such a vision is to be pondered as profoundly tragic or dismissed with an ironic shrug depends ultimately on the reader. As the eagle says, 'Take yt in ernest or in game' (822).[37]

The larger meaning of the poem, like its ending, is also a mat-ter of controversy (see the Riverside edition, 977–8). If we confine ourselves here to the question asked before (viz. how does the

Virgilian material in Book 1 fit into the general scheme of the poem?) we may now be in a position to give a more precise answer. In discussing Book 1 we noticed several conceptions which may be listed as follows: (1) Venus as a loving mother, intervening not always necessarily or wisely on behalf of her son; (2) Venus as the goddess of romantic passion; (3) Aeneas as a callous traitor; (4) Aeneas as, eventually, the self-sacrificing servant of god; (5) Dido as an ill-used and suffering woman; and (6) Dido as one who, led astray by foolish desire, trusted a stranger too soon. Taken together, all these conceptions represent various and sometimes conflicting tidings about love, conveyed in one of the most celebrated of all love stories. That story, in which rumour plays a cardinal role, transmits the reputation of the participants – an ambiguous reputation which, thanks to the quality of the poem, has ensured their lasting renown. It need only be added that one Latin word encompasses tidings, story, rumour, reputation, and renown, viz. *fama*. That, surely, is what Chaucer meant by Fame.[38]

In *The Legend of Good Women* Chaucer used heroic couplets for the first time. These gave him more scope than the octosyllabic line of *The House of Fame*. At the same time they lent a more rapid movement to the narrative than the rhyme royal stanzas which he had used in *Troilus and Criseyde*. In recounting the legend of Dido, Chaucer has little interest in the *Aeneid* as such. The events of Book 2 are quickly summarized to provide a background, and Book 3 is covered in nine lines, of which three point out its irrelevance. In the story of Dido and Aeneas the supernatural element is played down. After revealing that the huntress who gives Aeneas directions is really Venus in disguise, Chaucer makes it clear that he is just following Virgil (1002). When Venus makes Aeneas invisible, Chaucer hints at his doubts (1020) and adds, 'Thus seyth the bok, withouten any les' (1022). When Dido first falls in love with Aeneas, nothing is said to suggest that her infatuation is caused by Venus (1075–9). When, in 1139ff., Venus substitutes Cupid for Ascanius (a piece of Virgilian symbolism), Chaucer detaches himself from the account (1139) and expresses his indifference quite openly:

> but, as of that scripture,
> Be as be may, I take of it no cure. (1144–5)   (notice)

More generally, in spite of a passing reference to Aeneas' destiny
(952) and to 'that God, that hevene and erthe made' (1039), we are
told that Fortune 'hath the world in governaunce' (1044). That is
no part of the epic's theology any more than of Christianity's.
The effect of all this is to present the love of Dido and Aeneas as
an independent romantic story which works itself out in purely
human terms.

   In relating it, Chaucer inserts passages of direct speech at crucial moments. As well as producing a vividly dramatic effect
(which was not attempted in *The House of Fame* except in Dido's
lament), these speeches shape the narrative in new and distinctive ways. In the *Aeneid*, when Aeneas notices the scenes from
the Trojan war in Dido's temple, he does, it is true, weep as he
ponders on the tragedy of his past (459, 465). Nevertheless, the
effect of the pictures is to give him fresh heart; for they show
that the Carthaginians too admire glorious deeds and are moved
by the sadness of human experience – the *lacrimae rerum* (461–2).
For Chaucer's Aeneas there is no encouragement. The scenes
simply reflect the disgrace of Troy's defeat. 'Allas, that I was
born!' he cries,

> 'No lenger for to lyven I ne kepe'   (care)
> And with that word he brast out for to wepe   (burst)
> So tenderly that routhe it was to sene. (1032–4) (pitiful)

Such unalloyed pathos, though it lacks the heroic resilience found
in Virgil, is at least genuine. Later, the implications of his tears
are more disagreeable. When Dido senses his uneasiness and asks
what is amiss, he tells her that Anchises and Mercury have been
urging him to sail to Italy. Since we have not heard Jupiter giving
Mercury his instructions (as we did in the *Aeneid*), Aeneas' assertions are left unsubstantiated and sound like fabrications. This
suspicion is confirmed when, unlike Virgil or Ovid, the narrator
adds on his own authority,

Therwith his false teres out they sterte,
And taketh hire withinne his armes two. (1301–2)

These touches reduce the hero's moral stature.

Dido's speeches bring a similar change of emphasis. When she confesses her love to her sister, she makes no mention of her dead husband and the loyalty he inspires (1170–81). Anna, for her part, tries to put her off, but fails, whereas in the *Aeneid* she gives sensible encouragement (and so, ironically, helps to precipitate the disaster). The result of this change (which is also a change from *HF* 369–71) is to imply that Dido's erotic-romantic impulse is uncomplicated by earlier attachments and strong enough to sweep aside whatever prudential arguments Anna may have adduced. Later, at the climax of her final appeal, Dido cries: 'I am with childe, and yeve my child his lyf!' (1323). In Virgil it is the *absence* of a *paruulus Aeneas* that increases Dido's pathos; in Ovid she hints at the possibility of a child in order to hold Aeneas back; here she claims its existence as a fact. By ignoring such an appeal Aeneas is still more utterly condemned.

So much for the speeches. A word now about Chaucer's descriptions, which situate the story in the medieval world, or at the very least blur the distinction between ancient and medieval. First there is the list of presents (unlike those in Virgil)[39] sent by the queen to Aeneas – coursers well bridled, steeds for jousting, palfreys, jewels, sacks of gold, falcons, hounds – all the sumptuous paraphernalia of a medieval court (1114ff.). The hounds point forward to Chaucer's description of the royal hunt (1190ff.) in which the picture of the queen herself is particularly impressive:

Upon a thikke palfrey, paper-whit,
With sadel red, enbrouded with delyt,
Of gold the barres up enbosed hye,
Sit Dido, al in gold and perre wrye.   (covered in jewellery)

Just such a procession is shown in *Les très riches heures du Duc de Berry* (for August).[40] There, some years after Chaucer's death, we have a lady on a white palfrey, accompanied by hounds and falcons. As for Dido's looks, Virgil simply calls her *forma pulcherrima Dido* (1.496). Chaucer elaborates splendidly:

> This noble queen that cleped was Dido, (called)
> That whilom was the wif of Sytheo,
> That fayrer was than is the bryghte sonne,
> This noble toun of Cartage hath bigonne;
> In which she regneth in so gret honour
> That she was holden of alle queenes flour
> Of gentillesse, of fredom, of beaute. (1004–10)

Again, whereas Virgil, prompted by *Odyssey* 6.102f., compares Dido to Diana leading the dance (1.498-504), Chaucer writes that the queen

> Stod in the temple in hire estat real,
> So rychely and ek so fayr withal,
> So yong, so lusty, with hire eyen glade,
> That, if that God, that hevene and erthe made,
> Wolde han a love, for beaute and goodnesse,
> And womanhod, and trouthe, and semelynesse,
> Whom shulde he loven but this lady swete? (1036–42)

Surely this is astonishing. It is one thing for a pagan to compare a woman to Diana, but quite another for a Christian poet to say that a certain woman would make a suitable love for God the creator.[41] But, however we explain this point, these passages will remind us that again and again in *LGW*, in contrast to *HF* and Ovid's *Epistle*, Chaucer insists on Dido's regal nobility. He also sees her as a pious lady. Admittedly Virgil's Dido is said to be building a temple in honour of Juno (1.446–7), but when we first see her she is dispensing law and justice (1.507). Chaucer's, however, is 'in hire devocyoun' (1017) – i.e., at prayer. Later, when abandoned, 'she seketh halwes' (1310), visiting holy shrines. The witchcraft, to which Virgil's Dido pretends to have recourse (4.478ff.), is completely omitted.

If Dido is like a medieval queen, Aeneas is

> lyk a knyght,
> And suffisaunt of persone and of myght
> And lyk to been a verray gentil man. (1066–8)

In the cave scene, which Chaucer no longer shirks as he did in
HF 245ff., Aeneas kneels and declares his love and woe in the
proper knightly fashion. And although, according to Chaucer, he
was totally insincere, Dido 'rewede [took pity on] his peyne'
(1237). The courtly convention did not allow ladies to seduce
gentlemen, or even to share in their pleasure; but they might
'take pity' on them, and give their consent as an act of mercy.
Shortly after, Chaucer gives a brilliant glimpse of a courtly lover
in action:

> This Troyan, that so wel hire plesen can,
> That feyneth hym so trewe and obeysynge,
> So gentil, and so privy of his doinge,   (discreet)
> And can so wel don alle his obeysaunces,   (acts of dutiful respect)
> And wayten hire at festes and at daunces,   (attend)
> And whan she goth to temple and hom ageyn,
> And fasten til he hath his lady seyn,
> And beren in his devyses, for hire sake,   (heraldic devices)
> Not I not what; and songes wolde he make,
> Justen, and don of armes many thynges,   (joust; perform; feats)
> Sende hire lettres, tokens, broches, rynges. (1265–75)

Then, after portraying Aeneas as a well-mannered and attentive
cad, Chaucer completes the effect as follows:

> This Eneas, that hath so depe yswore,
> Is wery of his craft withinne a throwe;   (tricks; short time)
> The hote ernest is al overblowe.   (passion; past)
> And pryvyly he doth his shipes dyghte,   (prepare)
> And shapeth hym to stele awey by nyghte. (1285–9)

This is quite contrary to the *Aeneid*. For Virgil makes it clear
that Aeneas is *not* tired of Dido, and also that he did *not* intend

to slink away without seeing her. What he says to his men is, in effect, this: 'Get the fleet ready as secretly as possible; when the moment is right I will speak to Dido' (4.289–94).[42]

A final illustration. As Jill Mann points out (39ff.), in the *Legend of Dido* (and, indeed, in *The Legend of Good Women* as a whole) women pity men, but not *vice versa*. In Virgil, however, this is not the case. As Aeneas is fond of Dido, he feels pity as well as other emotions: *lenire dolentem solando cupit* (4.393–4), 'he longs to soothe her distress by comforting her'; and after that moving scene in the underworld *prosequitur lacrimis longe et miseratur euntem* (6.476), 'he gazes tearfully after her from afar, and pities her as she departs.'[43] Chaucer wants none of this. The fact is that he is not interested in Aeneas and his inward struggles. The same is true of Ovid. But Ovid confined himself to presenting Dido's thoughts about Aeneas. He did not, as author, make any assertions on his own. So, strictly, Chaucer does not follow either Virgil or Ovid here; he goes well beyond both.

As with *HF*, Book 1, Chaucer ends by referring to Virgil and Ovid. But this time he gives an account of Dido's death (condensed from *Aeneid* 4), and a free translation of the opening of the *Epistle*. The translation does, it is true, reproduce two pieces of Ovid's word-play (on 'lose' and 'blow'), but the effect is less obtrusive, in that Chaucer supplies two instances, and then stops after eight lines; whereas Ovid (if we read *mouimus* in line 4) gives six instances in fourteen. It is a matter of degree.

The slant of the legend, in particular the favourable presentation of the queen – so beautiful and noble, and so grievously wronged – and the denigration of Aeneas, must be connected in some way with the context of the collection as a whole. This raises a number of questions which I am happy to evade. Is the original plan complete? If not, is that because Chaucer became bored? Why are there two versions of the Prologue, and what are their different functions? Why is the daisy celebrated with such enthusiasm? Who or what lies behind the figure of Alceste? Such questions are for experts to wrestle with. A visitor ought not to meddle. Even the question of why Chaucer wrote *The Legend of Good Women* is hard to answer. The literal truth is wrapped in a dream; which means that Chaucer did not wish his readers to know the (perhaps rather prosaic) details. *Within* the dream the God of Love accuses Chaucer of slandering lovers and making people distrust him (249–53); by translating the *Romance of the Rose* he has implied that a person who loves 'to harde and hote' is an absolute fool (258–60); and by recounting how Criseyde forsook Troilus he has shown 'how that women han doth mis' (265–6). Obviously most of the accusations are open to question. The same is true of most of the pleas put forward by Alceste in mitigation. What does emerge, in general terms, is that *LGW* is supposed in some way to redress the balance by depicting famous cases of good women who were wronged by men. As the God says:

> Why noldest thow as wel seyd goodnesse
> Of wemen, as thow hast seyd wikednesse? (268–9)

So much we are asked to accept for the sake of the poet's fiction. But the question remains – and even a visitor must face up to this – how are we meant to *take* the poem? The series of blameless and suffering women has been too much for some modern scholars.[44] The worldly-wise Chaucer, they say, could never have written such simple stuff; he must be tipping his readers a satirical wink. Yet this seems to be based partly on a fallacy and partly on a misconception of Chaucer's rhetoric. The fallacy lies in the contention that, if an assertion is plainly only half true, the opposite must be intended. But no one imagines that because 'many hands make light work' is only half true, 'too many cooks spoil the broth' must be universally valid. Sweeping generalizations are simply a form of overstatement, which is one way of imparting emphasis. Granted, there are also two other ways – understatement and irony (i.e. saying the opposite of what you mean). But rhetorical generalization is what we are dealing with here; we have already met it in the epigram *uarium et mutabile semper femina*.

An analogy is at hand in what the Prologue says about 'olde bokes.' Since the stories that are about to be told are drawn from antiquity, Chaucer wishes to stress that they should be taken seriously. He therefore constructs an argument starting from the valid point that we should not *dis*believe a story simply because it is found in an ancient text which cannot be checked (G 12–13). He then moves on to the much more sweeping, and quite *in*valid, assertion that we should believe old books because there is no way of verifying them (G 27–8, 83–4). But then he retreats from this position, saying, in effect, that he intends to present the bare stories told by earlier writers: 'leveth hem if yow leste' (88), 'believe them if you wish'.

Much later the God of Love chides the poet for writing about women's 'unstedefastnesse,' saying 'thow knowest here goodnesse / By pref, and ek by storyes herebyforn' (527–8). So it seems that there are at least certain general truths in old books which can be checked from experience. Yet here again we are dealing with a rhetorical generalization; for women's 'goodnesse,' at first sight anyhow, seems to mean *all* women's goodnesse. It is not until the next line that the worthlessness of some women is conceded; even then the balance is tilted in favour of virtue:

Let be the chaf, and writ wel of the corn.

Similarly, the God of Love had claimed earlier that classical writers told of a hundred good women for every one bad (274–7).

Returning to the legends, then, all we are asked to believe in the end is that loyalty (which in this context is the female virtue *par excellence*)[45] is typical of the majority of women. This, Chaucer hopes, will readily offset the inference (if anyone ever drew it) that the *dis*loyalty of Criseyde is typical of the majority of women. Those who contest this straightforward interpretation point to the characters of Cleopatra and Medea; surely, by suppressing their crimes and vices Chaucer must really be calling attention to them. But, as all the women illustrate the same quality, we must then discover crimes and / or vices in the others too; and that cannot be done. Even if we leave aside crime and vice, and think only of folly, *LGW* offers virtually no support to the cynical ironists. In *HF*, to be sure, Dido did not escape censure for her foolish desire (287–8). But no similar judgment is passed in *LGW*. We are told that Anna's objections were not heeded; but instead of condemning Dido's folly, Chaucer simply says in 1186–7

> But finaly, it may nat ben withstonde;
> Love wol love, for nothing wol it wonde.   (cease)

Nor are the other good women presented as foolish. In two cases, indeed, folly is ruled out by the very nature of the story; for Lucretia and Philomela were not seduced but raped. Finally, at a point when Chaucer might have dwelt on women's folly had that been his intention, he put instead a general and very gentle question:

> O sely wemen, ful of innocence,   (hapless)
> Ful of pite, of trouthe and conscience,
> What maketh yow to men to truste so? (1254–6)

As in antiquity, so in Chaucer's day an author was entitled to suppress what he wanted his readers to overlook.[46] We have seen how in *LGW* Chaucer 'edited' Virgil's account of Dido and Aeneas. He applied the same process to Cleopatra and Medea. As Cleopatra was loyal to Antony, and Medea did not betray Jason, that was all Chaucer needed. Their other actions (even though in Medea's case these amounted to enormities) could be ignored.

If this argument is correct, then however light-hearted Chaucer may be towards his courtly readers, he is not laughing up his sleeve at his heroines; he is just employing them to illustrate in simple primary colours the contention that most women are faithful. Could he, one wonders, have cited a parallel list of cases in favour of men?[47]

CHAPTER TWO

Shakespeare and Plautus
Two Twin Comedies

In comparing the two plays I shall quickly outline the *Menaechmi*,
noting certain features.[1] Then, going on to *The Comedy of Errors*,
I shall describe how, while retaining important Plautine elements,
Shakespeare wove the Latin farce into the framework of a Hellenistic romance, and how in doing so he developed both genres into
something richer and more complex, something which reflected
contemporary ideas on love and on Christian marriage.

The background of the *Menaechmi* is supplied in the ingratiat-
ingly jokey prologue.[2] A father from Syracuse takes one twin to
Tarentum and leaves the other at home. At Tarentum, the boy
Menaechmus gets lost in the crowd and is carried off to Epidamnus by a merchant. Though the father dies of a broken heart, in
Epidamnus the boy is well brought up, and eventually a wife is
found for him, complete with dowry. After this the kidnapper is
conveniently drowned – a death described in suitably heartless
terms.[3] Back in Sicily the grandfather changed the second twin's
name to Menaechmus in order to maintain the family tradition.
Years later, Menaechmus 2 sets off in search of his brother and
eventually comes to Epidamnus.

The speaker of the Prologue has by now given the author's
name (Plautus), cajoled the audience into a receptive mood, out-
lined the events leading up to the play, and in general made
possible a smooth transition from the real-life theatre in Rome to
the imaginary setting of Epidamnus on the coast of the modern
Albania. He concludes with a gesture towards the simple, all-
purpose, set:

haec urbs Epidamnus est dum haec agitur fabula:
quando alia agetur aliud fiet oppidum (72–3)

This city is Epidamnus as long as this play is in progress;[4]
when another play is on, it will become another town.

The play proper begins with the entrance of the parasite Peniculus, who at once introduces himself: 'The young set call me
Brush, because when I eat I sweep the table clean.'[5] He then
delivers a homily on how to keep friends. Briefly, you bind them
to you by food and drink:

apud mensam plenam homini rostrum deliges (89)

You should fasten a fellow's snout to a full table.

If you do, then he'll never run away, even if he has committed
murder. Now comes the practical illustration. Peniculus is going
to visit his friend and patron Menaechmus, who has exactly that
kind of hold over his affections. In fact Menaechmus' table is
piled so high that if you want something off the top you have to
stand on your chair. Clearly the purpose of all this is to prepare
us for the main character, who is something of a glutton. And
that, in turn, provides an introduction to the business of *cena*,
or 'dinner,' which has such an important part in the action.
That importance is greatly reduced by Shakespeare, who has
other dramatic interests. And so it is no surprise to find that
Peniculus the gormandizer has no counterpart in *The Comedy of
Errors*.

Menaechmus now enters, abusing his wife, who is indoors and
has presumably switched him off:

nam quotiens foras ire uolo, me retines, reuocas, rogitas
quo ego eam, quam rem agam, quid negoti geram,
quid petam, quid feram, quid foris egerim. (114–16)

The succession of dactyls and cretics conveys his exasperation –
an effect lost in a prose rendering:

> When I want to go out, you call me back and delay me, asking
> where I'm going, what I'm doing, what I'm engaged in, what I'm
> after, what I've got, what I've been up to downtown.

He concludes: 'I've got a customs-officer in the house; for I have
to declare everything.' Much later in the play, the wife (who by
then has ample reason to be angry) sees Menaechmus in the
street. 'How should I handle him?' she asks Peniculus (568). 'In
the same way as usual,' says Peniculus. 'Pitch into him!' This
confirms our view of the *matrona* as a scold. One thinks of her
as being rather like the cartoon figure Andy Capp's wife, with
hair in curlers and brandishing a rolling pin. So there is no sense
of outrage when at the end of the play Menaechmus decides to
auction her off with the rest of his effects, if he can find a bidder.
Plautus, therefore, does not intend for a moment that the character should engage our sympathy.

And this turns out to be entirely appropriate; for Menaechmus
has no moral status either. He has reacted to his wife's nagging
by stealing one of her dresses; and as the play opens he is on his
way to present it to his girlfriend Erotium, 'Sexpot,' a prostitute
who lives near by. It then becomes clear that Menaechmus has
not only stolen the dress; he is actually wearing it under his
cloak. The scene now turns into a farcical drag act, as Menaechmus minces around the stage, showing off to Peniculus, and
preening himself on his squalid piece of thievery. (At one point
in all this horseplay Menaechmus and Peniculus go so far as to
smell the dress. As Erich Segal says, Plautus is rarely as unsavoury as this.)[6] In due course the dress is presented to Erotium,
who turns out to be a good deal more than a common tart. She
has her own establishment where she can give dinner parties; she
keeps a maid; and she is used to giving orders to a cook. Again,
as Erotium is not quite the conventional tart, she does not have
a heart of gold. Peniculus wryly comments that her affability is
just a façade (193ff.). Granted his viewpoint is suspect, because he
hates to see Menaechmus waste money on *her* which could be
spent on feeding *him*. Yet his cynical verdict on Erotium is confirmed when, after receiving the dress, she immediately plans to

enhance its value by getting Menaechmus to pay for alterations (426–7). She then tells her maid to persuade him to add an ounce of gold to a bracelet stolen on a previous occasion from his wife (526–32). Finally her maid gets into the act by wheedling Menaechmus into throwing in a pair of gold earrings for *her* (541–3).

So by the end of Act 1 we have a nagging wife, a deceitful and clownish husband, a gluttonous parasite, and a mercenary whore. What a collection! But really Plautus is not inviting us to condemn these characters. For to condemn them we should first have to take them seriously as moral beings. In fact they are little more than broad stereotypes. And that is fine for the sort of comedy which we are being offered – one which presents a few two-dimensional figures as victims of a series of farcical misconceptions.

These misconceptions begin with the arrival of the Syracusan Menaechmus, whom I shall refer to as 'the Seeker.' The Seeker is accompanied by his slave Messenio, who gravely warns him about the deplorable reputation of Epidamnus, or Ruinville:

> huic urbi nomen Epidamno inditumst,
> quia nemo ferme huc sine damno deuortitur. (263–4)

> This town is called Ruinville, because pretty well no one stays here without being ruined.

In this den of trickery, then, the Seeker is mistaken for his brother, first by the cook, then by Erotium, then by Peniculus, and then by Erotium's maid. That takes us to the end of Act 3. It is worth adding that the Seeker is morally a true twin of his brother; for having dined and had sex with Erotium on a completely false basis, he promises to have trimmings added to her dress, and extra gold put on her bracelet, while all the time intending to sell these articles as soon as he goes downtown (549).

Meanwhile Peniculus, detained by a public meeting, has been done out of his dinner. This has proved too much for his loyalty, and he has told Menaechmus' wife about the theft. Eventually, in Act 5, she catches Menaechmus with the dress; but alas it is the wrong Menaechmus. As a result of the ensuing row, she sends for her father, who concludes that his son-in-law has gone off his head. Seizing on this as a possible way of escape, the Seeker pretends to be raving mad, whereupon the father goes to fetch a doctor. By the time *he* arrives (late, of course, and full of pretentious jargon) the assumed patient has been replaced by Menaechmus. After further altercation, Menaechmus is led away, but is rescued in a brawl by Messenio, who mistakes him for his master. Finally the two Menaechmi encounter each other, and (surprise surprise) Messenio realizes they are twin brothers. Following the recognition scene Messenio is given his freedom – an act of poetic justice towards the only half-decent character among the main actors.[7]

On turning to *The Comedy of Errors*, the first thing to notice is the absence of a Prologue. We are plunged *in medias res*, and the background is supplied piecemeal by the characters themselves. The scene is Ephesus on the coast of Asia Minor, and the circumstances are grim indeed. Egeon, a merchant from Syracuse, is under sentence of death unless he can raise 1,000 marks in ransom money. The reason is that Ephesus and Syracuse are in a state of conflict, which involves reprisals, though not actual war. This conflict presupposes a larger, political, background, which is not present in the *Menaechmi*. More important, the geographical background is also much wider. In the *Menaechmi*, Syracuse, Tarentum, and Epidamnus form a relatively small triangle, intelligible and indeed familiar to a Roman audience. But the English audience would have had only the haziest idea about the location of Syracuse, Epidamnum, and Ephesus. Still, for reasons which I shall mention shortly, they had all heard of Ephesus; and so they listened as the hapless Egeon told his story.

When sailing home from Epidamnum to Syracuse, Egeon and his family were shipwrecked and, as a result, separated. The family consisted of his wife, their twin sons, and *their* twin servants: six in all. Egeon, with son Antipholus and servant Dromio, eventually got back to Syracuse. Many years later Antipholus sets off with Dromio to search for his twin and also for his mother:

> So I, to find a mother and a brother,
> In quest of them, unhappy, lose myself. (1.2.39–40)

Egeon, too, keeps making enquiries as he travels round the eastern Mediterranean on business.[8] Foakes speaks of 'the measured
dignity' and 'simple gravity' of Egeon's tale. As the man himself
is doomed, the situation ought to be tragic. Yet this doesn't seem
quite right, as the play has been advertised as a comedy. By the
end of the scene the answer will have been clear, at least to the
more alert. Though Egeon's ship went down in a storm, he and
his family survived by lashing themselves to a mast. When they
were about to be saved, the mast was split in two by a rock; yet
they still remained afloat. Half the company was picked up by a
fishing boat from Corinth, and the other half by a ship bound for
Syracuse. Such miraculous escapes belong to a genre which has
the pains and ordeals of tragedy but the happy ending of comedy
– namely, the romance.

We now jump ahead to Act 5. The recognitions begin when
Egeon, on his way to execution, sees the Ephesian Antipholus and
Dromio, whom he wrongly takes to be the two from Syracuse
(5.1.195–6). Soon, however, the two Antipholuses and the two
Dromios come together; and all is concluded, if not explained,
when the abbess of the priory at Ephesus enters. For she turns
out to be none other than Emilia, Egeon's long-lost wife, and
mother of the Antipholus twins. Egeon is duly set free, and in
true comic fashion they all go off to supper. So, whereas in the
Menaechmi the comedy is preceded by a prologue – Prologue /
Comedy – in Shakespeare's play the comedy is woven into a
framework of romance – Romance / Comedy / Romance.[9]

Although not traditionally acknowledged in classical sylla-
buses,[10] the sentimental romance evolved as a literary form in the
Graeco-Roman world. As with other genres, its origins are controversial; and fortunately they do not concern us here. Enough to
recall that five specimens have survived, and that we have fragments of many more. Set in the eastern Mediterranean, they have
to do with fine, handsome young men and beautiful modest girls,
who are separated at the beginning of the story and are finally
reunited after the most hair-raising adventures. The events in
Xenophon of Ephesus' *Ethiopian Story* are summarized thus by
Paul Turner in the introduction to his translation (1957): 'Anthea
is captured by pirates, nearly raped, nearly made a human sacri-

fice, buried alive after she has drugged herself to avoid a distasteful marriage, buried in a pit with two fierce dogs. Yet she ends up none the worse for her adventures. Meanwhile Habrocomes her husband has been shipwrecked off the coast of Egypt, captured by shepherds, sold into slavery, falsely accused of murdering his master, crucified on a rock overlooking the Nile, swept by a gale into the river; fished out again and condemned to be burnt at the stake. Happily thc Nile overflows and puts out the flames; and Habrocomes is spared for a new series of surprising experiences.' From this it will be inferred that credibility is not the genre's strongest feature.

A few of these romances, notably those of Achilles Tatius, Longus, and Heliodorus, were known in England at a surprisingly early date, mainly in versions of Latin or French translations.[11] But the most influential of all was one which had disappeared much earlier. Before it was lost, an adaptation had been made in Latin under the title *Historia Apollonii Regis Tyri*, usually shortened to *Apollonius of Tyre*.[12] Towards the end of this work Apollonius, thanks to a dream, eventually travels to Ephesus, where he is reunited with his wife, now priestess of the Temple of Diana in that city. The work came down through the Middle Ages in several versions.[13] The one known to Shakespeare was in Book 8 of John Gower's poem *Confessio Amantis* (1390), where Apollonius' wife, Lucina, is significantly called an abbesse (1849). Did her name suggest Luciana's? Possibly; but at any rate Shakespeare was interested enough in the story to use it again in *Pericles Prince of Tyre*.

The procedure of sandwiching a farce of mistaken identity between the concluding scenes of a romance was heavily criticized by Quiller-Couch: 'As yet farce and romance were not one "form" but two separate stools; and between them in *The Comedy of Errors* [Shakespeare] fell to the ground.'[14] Yet in view of its continued popularity the play cannot be written off as a failure; and so it is worth looking more closely at the ways in which the two different genres have been brought together. We have already seen that improbabilities of plot were no obstacle. What, then, about the social rank of the participants? The Latin title of the romance shows that the hero was a prince; and his wife was a princess, daughter of King Archestrates of Pentapolis in Cyrenaica (North Africa). There is nothing, however, to connect Shakespeare's Egeon with the aristocracy. He is simply a merchant from Syracuse. His son, the Syracusan Antipholus, is on the same level (1.2); and the Ephesian twin also appears to be in trade (2.1.4–5, 11). So Shakespeare has eliminated the discrepancy of class by setting his play in the same world as that of the Menaechmi, who were sons of a Syracusan merchant (17).

Within this bourgeois world four types of connection are established. First, a neat link is provided in 1.2.3–7 when a merchant informs the newly arrived Antipholus that

> This very day a Syracusian merchant
> Is apprehended for arrival here,
> And not being able to buy out his life,
> According to the statutes of the town
> Dies ere the weary sun set in the west.

Towards the end of the play (5.1.124–8) a second merchant says to Adriana (the Ephesian Antipholus' wife) and her friends that the Duke is coming

> To see a reverend Syracusian merchant,
> Who put unluckily into the bay
> Against the laws and statutes of this town,
> Beheaded publicly for his offence.

So at the opening and at the finish of the play Egeon is presented to the others as a fellow merchant.

Second, in 1.2 the local merchant, on greeting Antipholus of Syracuse, says 'There is your money that I had to keep.' Antipholus hands it to his servant Dromio. Later (1.2.81), when he asks to have it back, the amount is said to be 1,000 marks – the exact sum which was needed to save Egeon's life (1.1.21). By reminding us of this point at 2.1.61 and 65, and again at 3.1.8, Shakespeare creates a vague undercurrent of suspense: if only Antipholus knew who Egeon was.

The most important illustration of what might be called

Shakespeare's mercantile emphasis is the fact that, unlike Plautus, he uses gold and sums of money as the chief instruments of misunderstanding. In the *Menaechmi*, as we saw, the main focus of confusion was the stolen dress. That, like the stolen bracelet, was a symbol of Menaechmus' infidelity. The wallet of money belonging to Menaechmus the Seeker (265, 385–6, 701–2, 1035–7) played a much smaller part in the complication of the plot. Shakespeare, however, makes important and recurrent use of the Syracusan's money (1.2.9; 1.2.54ff.; 2.1.61ff.; 2.2.1), of the golden chain promised to Adriana, the Ephesian's wife (2.1.106; 3.1.1; 3.1.114ff.; 3.2.165ff.; 4.1.1ff.; 4.3.45; 4.4.133; 5.1.2ff.), and of the ducats sent by Adriana to secure the Ephesian's freedom (4.1.103; 2.42; 3.12; 4.11; 4.81ff.). All these items cause confusion and altercation, with frequent charges of bad faith and dishonesty. Shakespeare, however, did not take over Plautus' dress, and he transformed the bracelet into a (more visible) chain, giving it a different and more complex function. Before leaving this commercial theme, we may perhaps risk a preliminary reference to St Paul who, as we are told in Acts 19, caused a riot by preaching the gospel in Ephesus. The trouble began among the silversmiths who made 'shrines' (ναούς) for the goddess Diana, and who understandably saw their livelihood threatened by this new religion. The silversmiths' craft, then, was one of the things that English people associated with Ephesus. So, although the point will not bear much weight, it is at least appropriate that in a play set in Ephesus Shakespeare should have created the character of Angelo the goldsmith and made an important comic motif out of a gold chain.[15]

The Ephesus of the Acts is also the centre of much stranger things. According to the *New English Bible*, 'through Paul God worked miracles of an unusual kind: when handkerchiefs and scarves which had been in contact with his skin were carried to the sick, they were rid of their diseases and the evil spirits came out of them.' Such miracles, no doubt, were accepted as authentic and unsinister by the Elizabethan reader. 'But,' continues the account, 'some strolling Jewish exorcists tried their hand at using the name of the Lord Jesus on those possessed by evil spirits; they would say, "I adjure you by Jesus whom Paul proclaims".

There were seven sons of Sceva, a Jewish chief priest, who were using this method, when the evil spirit answered back and said, "Jesus I acknowledge, and I know about Paul, but who are you?" And the man with the evil spirit flew at them, overpowered them all, and handled them with such violence that they ran out of the house stripped and battered. This became known to everybody in Ephesus ... Moreover many of those who had become believers came and openly confessed that they had been using magical spells. And a good many of those who formerly practised magic collected their books and burnt them publicly' (Acts 19.11–19). Now the *Menaechmi* is almost completely lacking in a supernatural dimension. When a character is bewildered he complains he is being mocked, or tricked, or insulted; or that another person is asleep, or dreaming, or drunk, or raving mad; but he hardly ever claims that the mysterious events are due to witchcraft.[16] In Shakespeare, however, a sequence of strange events reveals the terrifying duality of the world – a world in which Satan and his followers are in perpetual revolt against God (even though they can never hope to win). This cosmic struggle is mirrored within the human soul, which at times of crisis is in danger of being overwhelmed by the forces of evil. When possessed, the human person ceases to be 'himself.' Having lost his identity he no longer controls his own actions; and he faces not only a life of madness on earth, but also eternal damnation in the world to come. Such anxieties are present in the Syracusan's mind when he describes the spiritual atmosphere of Ephesus:

> They say this town is full of cozenage,
> As nimble jugglers that deceive the eye,
> Dark-working sorcerers that change the mind,
> Soul-killing witches that deform the body. (1.2.97–100)

These suspicions seem to be borne out by the happenings which follow. Fascinated by Adriana's sister, Luciana, who unaccountably knows his name, the Syracusan concludes, only half-figuratively, that she must be a siren (3.2.47) or a mermaid (163); the town seems to be inhabited by witches (3.2.155) and sorcerers

(4.3.12). So when the Courtesan accosts the Syracusan pair, using the right name, they look on her as an incarnation of the devil (4.3.43ff.). These fears are not confined to the Syracusans. The womenfolk are convinced that the Ephesian Antipholus is out of his wits, and so bring in Dr Pinch to conjure or exorcise the evil spirit.[17] He duly intones

> I charge thee, Satan, hous'd within this man,
> To yield possession to my holy prayers,
> And to thy state of darkness hie thee straight;
> I conjure thee by all the saints in heaven. (4.4.52–5)

This marks a significant elaboration of the *Menaechmi*, in which the doctor (though no more effective) enquires about the patient's fluid intake, and whether he suffers from flatulence; he then undertakes to give him a course of hellebore (915ff.).[18] In these scenes, then, Shakespeare has taken only the slightest hint from the *Menaechmi*. He is much more indebted to the Acts, a source quite outside the area of the comedy, which he has exploited to enhance the farce.[19]

He also uses the Acts to weave the farce into the framework of a now Christianized romance. For when the 'deranged' Antipholus of Syracuse moves out of the Plautine comedy into the closing scenes of the play, he is taken in hand by Emilia, a serious figure who promises to treat the patient by all her 'approved means,' both physical and spiritual:

> With wholesome syrops, drugs and holy prayers
> To make of him a formal man again. (5.1.104–5)

So the mind will be restored to normality by one who is no longer the priestess of a pagan temple, but a Christian abbess using Christian procedures.

As Shakespeare developed the outer frame into something more than romance, so he developed the inner play into something more than farce. To see how, we shall first look briefly at the Antipholus twins, contrasting them with the Menaechmi. At the beginning of Plautus' comedy, Menaechmus has been driven out of the house by his nagging wife, and as a reprisal he resolves to visit Erotium:

> atque adeo, ne me nequiquam serues, ob eam industriam
> hodie ducam scortum ad cenam atque aliquo condicam foras (123–4)

In other words, 'I'll give you something to be suspicious about; I'll have dinner with a floozie' (*scortum* is a low word). Later it transpires that this is no isolated incident. Menaechmus is a familiar client of Erotium's, and she is more than a dinner partner (358f.). Again, no secret is made of their liaison; evidently there is nothing very remarkable about it. When the wife's father comes on the scene, he takes the side of his son-in-law against his daughter, whom he rebukes for being unduly possessive. In exasperation she finally says, 'But look, he's having sex with a prostitute next door!' (790). Disconcertingly, the father answers, 'And he's jolly well right. Thanks to your interference he'll go there all the more often.' After hearing more in the same vein the wife remarks with some bitterness, 'I see I've brought you here, Father, to plead my husband's case, not mine. You're supposed to be on my side, but you're taking his.'

So much for Menaechmus. What about the Ephesian Antipholus? We know that his wife feels neglected. She complains to her sister when he fails to come home for dinner (2.1). But her trouble is more serious than this; for she has convinced herself that he is sleeping with another woman (2.1.108). In the next scene, in a highly emotional speech, she accuses Antipholus to his face of betraying her. Not surprisingly, she fails to get a satisfactory response because it is the wrong Antipholus. Meanwhile, her real husband is in Angelo's shop, seeing about a present for his wife. He is late for dinner (we are not told why), and he knows he is in for trouble.[20] So he asks Angelo to cover for him:

> My wife is shrewish when I keep not hours;
> Say that I linger'd with you at your shop
> To see the making of her carcanet. (3.1.2–4)

Eventually Antipholus, with his servant Dromio and his friend Balthasar, arrives home for dinner to find that he has been locked out. Inside, Adriana is dining with the Syracusan, whom she takes to be her husband. The row begins when the Syracusan Dromio, who is stationed inside, behind the door, exchanges abuse with his twin. Then the taunts are taken up by Luciana's maid; and finally Adriana herself appears for a brief moment – just long enough to send her husband packing

> *Ephesian Antipholus* Are you there, wife? You might have
>
> come before.
> *Adriana* Your wife, sir knave? Go, get you from the door!
>
> (3.1.63–4)

After rounding off the couplet, she flounces out, leaving Antipholus fuming with suspicion. Balthasar persuades him not to make a rumpus by breaking down the door with a crowbar; but Antipholus insists on registering a protest:

> I know a wench of excellent discourse,
> Pretty and witty; wild and yet, too, gentle;
> There will we dine. This woman that I mean,
> My wife (but I protest without desert)
> Hath oftentimes upbraided me withal;
> To her we will to dinner. (3.1.109–14)

So Antipholus asserts that he has gone to the woman because she is good company, and that (in spite of his wife's suspicions) he has not slept with her. If Shakespeare had meant to cast doubt on this, he could have done so through an expression of polite surprise on the part of Balthasar. But he lets the assertion stand; so for the moment one is inclined to give Antipholus the benefit of the doubt. In spite of his quick temper and his thoughtless lack of punctuality, Antipholus is therefore perceptibly superior to Menaechmus, who was a glutton, a liar, a thief, and a fornicator.

We shall see in a moment how the Ephesian Antipholus gradually moves beyond the Plautine romp. But first let us think for a moment about that exclusion scene. As usual, hints were supplied by the *Menaechmi*. In 661 Menaechmus submissively promises to return the dress to his wife. She says, in effect, 'You'd better; otherwise you won't be let into the house' (662). Menaechmus now has to retrieve the dress from Erotium. He is confident she will hand it over when he promises to buy her a nice new one, and that, so far from shutting him out, she will shut him in with her (671). But Erotium turns out to be much less obliging, and slams the door in his face (698). All this put Shakespeare in mind of the boisterous, but sadly fragmentary, scene in Plautus' *Amphitruo*, where the hero is shut out of his own house by Mercury while Jupiter is inside with Alcmena, Amphitruo's wife (1018ff.). On the basis of that scene Shakespeare created something quite new. The episode is cleverly prepared as the Ephesian and Balthasar walk home, looking forward to a belated dinner. The host modestly hopes that the food will be up to the occasion, and the guest assures him that the welcome is what really matters (3.1.19–29). Such civilities end abruptly when the door is found to be locked. There follows an interchange of lively abuse, full of the quibbles and bawdiness that Shakespeare and his audience loved. So here, following the ancient procedure of *aemulatio*, Shakespeare has taken on Plautus and in certain respects beaten him at his own game. For instance, when the Ephesian shouts for his maids,

Maud, Bridget, Marian, Cicely, Gillian, Ginn! (3.1.31),

the Syracusan Dromio, from behind the locked door, improvises a jeering retort in a similar metre:

Mome, malthorse, capon, coxcomb, idiot, patch!

The exchanges develop into classical stichomythia as one line answers another. And each riposte gains further sharpness when Shakespeare makes it the second member of a rhymed couplet:

Ephesian Dromio What patch is made our porter? My master
stays in the street.

> *Syracusan Dromio* Let him walk from whence he came, lest
> he catch cold on's feet.
> *Ephesian Antipholus* Who talks within there? ho, open the
> door.
> *Syracusan Dromio* Right, sir, I'll tell you when, and you'll tell
> me wherefore.
> *Ephesia Antipholus* Wherefore? for my dinner; I have not dined
> today.
> *Syracusan Dromio* Nor today here you must not; come again
> when you may. (36–41)

Again, as the altercation develops, Shakespeare brings in five different participants. This free-for-all is made possible because the focus has been moved from Amphitruo's bedroom to Antipholus' dining-room. In its new setting, and with its new characters, the exclusion scene has lost its element of theological burlesque, and with it the underlying bawdiness of its situation.[21] Nevertheless, it anchors the Ephesian Antipholus firmly within the context of a Plautine farce.

But as the play progresses, Antipholus begins to acquire another dimension. From the Syracusan's speech in 4.3 we infer that his twin is a popular figure in the city:

> There's not a man I meet but does salute me
> As if I were their well-acquainted friend,
> And everyone doth call me by my name:
> Some tender money to me, some invite me,
> Some other give me thanks for kindnesses,
> Some offer me commodities to buy. (1–6)

More evidence in favour of Antipholus is supplied in Act 5 by Angelo, who says he is a man

> Of very reverend reputation ...
> Of credit infinite, highly belov'd,
> Second to none that lives here in the city. (5.1.5–7)

More evidence still comes from the Duke, who (somewhat to our surprise) tells Adriana 'Long since thy husband serv'd me in my wars' (5.1.61); this is subsequently elaborated by Antipholus himself, who reminds the Duke how he once protected him on the battlefield:

> When I bestrid thee in the wars, and took
> Deep scars to save thy life. (5.1.192–3)

So the closer he comes to meeting his father, the nobler and less farcical Antipholus is made to appear.

We now come to the Syracusan Antipholus. He also belongs to two literary worlds. Though more dignified than Menaechmus the Seeker, he becomes the primary victim of comic error. Perhaps understandably, his reason is not able to cope with all that happens, and, as noted above, he concludes that the entire city is bewitched. His comic status is also shown by the verbal foolery which he carries on with the two Dromios. His status in the romance, on the other hand, is shown by his rapturous courtship of Luciana (3.2.29ff.). To span these two worlds, Shakespeare has given him a suitably elastic character.

When he first appears (1.2), he tells Dromio to go to the inn with the money. Dromio jokes: 'many a man would take the money and go for good.' As Dromio exits, Antipholus describes him as 'a trusty villain' – a phrase in which 'trusty' – is seriously meant and 'villain' is just good-natured banter. A little later, after an altercation with Dromio's twin, Antipholus concludes that his servant has allowed himself to be cheated out of the cash:

> Upon my life, by some device or other
> The villain is o'er-raught of all my money. (1.2.95–6)

This time, 'villain' is seriously meant, and Dromio's trustworthiness has apparently evaporated. Before we look at the comic scene which causes the change-around, let us go back again to Antipholus' description of Dromio:

> A trusty villain sir, that very oft,
> When I am dull with care and melancholy,
> Lightens my humour with his merry jests. (1.2.19–21)

So there is a gloomy side to Antipholus' character – one which we hear of half way through the scene:

> He that commends me to my own content
> Commends me to the thing I cannot get. (1.2.33-4)

In a famous simile, Antipholus goes on to compare himself to a drop of water which is lost in the ocean. As so often, the germ of the idea is found in the *Menaechmi*, where Messenio exclaims that the two twins are as alike as one drop of water (or milk) to another (1089). But Shakespeare uses the image to adumbrate the serious motif of the fluid self, which may be (regrettably) lost in the mass of humanity or (agreeably) merged with the self of a loved one. At present the gloomy sense predominates, for up to now Antipholus' quest has been futile, and he is in low spirits. So already the Syracusan is a more rounded figure than his Plautine prototype.

Yet this melancholy mood can, we are told, be lightened by Dromio's wit. So when Antipholus meets the wrong Dromio (1.2.41ff.) and obtains a sequence of absurd replies, he assumes his servant is trying to cheer him up. But at present he is not amenable to jokes and so reacts angrily (58, 68, 72, 80). As the bewildered Ephesian Dromio continues to talk nonsense, Antipholus loses his temper and begins to beat him: 'There, take you that, sir knave!' (92).

After 2.1, which is arranged in the sequence serious (1–43), comic (44–85), serious (86-116), Antipholus of Syracuse meets his *own* Dromio in 2.2. Still angry, he beats him once more for joking at the wrong moment. But a change of mood is signalled when Antipholus asks 'But say, sir, is it dinner-time?' (54).[22] A series of riddles and puns ensues during which Antipholus is coaxed into good humour in the very way described in 1.2.19–21 (quoted above); he is even given the satisfaction of having the last word (2.2.107). So these two comic encounters have a chiastic structure in that the first moves from good humour to anger and beating, and the second moves the other way.

In the dialogue between Luciana and the Syracusan (3.2) the romantic side of the latter's personality is fully revealed. I offer a paraphrase of the first sixteen lines of his speech (29–44): 'In your knowledge (as proved by your use of my name) and in your beauty you represent no less of a marvel than the earth itself; in fact you are more divine than anything earthly. Explain to my dull understanding the inner meaning of your puzzling words (i.e., 1–28). Why are you trying to baffle my soul which can apprehend the truth (viz. that we are meant for each other)? If you are a divinity, transform me and I shall become your slave. If I am who I *think* I am, then your sister is not my wife. It is to you that I am drawn.' Antipholus speaks of Luciana as a mermaid or siren, and longs to drown in her embrace (51) – a more explicitly erotic kind of self-surrender. Then, in language of quasi-religious adoration, he hails her as

> Mine eye's clear eye, my dear heart's dearer heart,
> My food, my fortune, and my sweet hope's aim,
> My sole earth's heaven, and my heaven's claim. (62–4)

Finally he begs her to be his wife.

The speech is comic in that the divine knowledge ascribed to Luciana is an illusion. Though she calls him by the right name (2), she is in error about his identity; and erring, as we know, is a human, not a divine habit. Moreover, Antipholus' language is amusing; for, although magnificent, it flies too high. This is the hyperbole of the infatuated, expressing a state which the world smiles at indulgently (and envies). Yet the speech projects feelings of sincere devotion, and this may suggest an analogy with the early scenes of a Greek romance before the lovers have been forced apart. Nevertheless, Shakespeare could not have found an impassioned address like that of Antipholus in his Greek sources. Likewise, though the Greek novels have certain religious overtones,[23] the Christian element in the speech ('My sole earth's heaven, and my heaven's claim') is not classical, but late Latin or medieval, in origin. This innovation corresponds to the metamorphosis of Diana's priestess (as found in the Apollonius romance) into the abbess of the priory.

Continuing to apply his technique of contrasts, Shakespeare now describes a very different scene of courtship – one which by

its grossness offers a parody of Antipholus' sentimental rap-
tures.[24] The narrator is the Syracusan Dromio, who comes on
stage panting (like the traditional *seruus currens*) after escaping
the attentions of Nell, Adriana's overweight kitchen maid. Antipholus here encourages, and enters into, the coarse humour of his
servant as he moves from the woman's fatness to her globe-like
figure, and from there to the countries located on her body.
Granted, there is more to this foolery than simple vulgarity; some
of the geographical references have a contemporary political
application.[25] Nevertheless, this scene shows once more the farcical aspect of Antipholus' personality.

Yet it is the serious Antipholus who remains at the end of the
play. After the 'deranged' comic victim has taken refuge with
Dromio in the priory he (like Egeon) is saved and returned to the
everyday world by the good offices of Emilia. But it is a happier
and more complete world, for Antipholus has found not only his
brother (as Menaechmus the Seeker did); he has also found his
parents, so that the play ends in a family reunion. And that is not
all. Though he can scarcely believe it, one of Antipholus' strange
experiences turns out not to have been an illusion, and this raises
hopes for a happy future. Addressing Luciana, he says

> What I told you then,
> I hope I shall have leisure to make good,
> If this be not a dream I see and hear. (5.1.374–6)

Before we leave the Antipholus twins, one more point should
be made about their sexual behaviour. During the exclusion scene
there is no suggestion that the Syracusan tries to take advantage
of Adriana, as Jupiter does with Alcmena in *Amphitruo*. He does
not find her attractive

> She that doth call me husband, even my soul
> Doth for a wife abhor (3.2.157–8);

and anyhow one assumes that he has eyes only for Luciana, who
is present throughout (2.1.6; 2.2.187 and 219; 5.1.207). Since
Adriana does not become sexually involved with the Syracusan,

her husband's wild suspicions are completely unfounded (4.4.57, 61, 99, 122; 5.1.197ff.). And even if she had, she would have been no more guilty than Alcmena, who acted out of ignorance. As for the Ephesian Antipholus, he has *not* attempted to seduce his sister-in-law, in spite of what Luciana and Adriana believe (4.2.1ff.). In financial matters, the Syracusan Dromio did *not* lose his master's money (1.2), and Angelo did *not* attempt to defraud the Ephesian Antipholus (4.1.49), or *vice versa*. The whole play is about misconceptions. Therefore, in spite of some doubts – doubts which are raised when Luciana later speaks of Antipholus 'demeaning himself' (5.1.87–8) – it would seem formally inappropriate if Adriana were right in accusing her husband of infidelity (3.1.111–13). If she is wrong, then all the sexual relationships in the play take place within the context of Christian courtship and marriage; even the much-mocked Nell pursues Dromio of Syracuse because she genuinely believes he is her fiancé (3.2.140, 154). As a result, Shakespeare, unlike Plautus, has no central role for the prostitute, and she dwindles into an anonymous minor figure.

We noted earlier how Shakespeare enhanced the farce by admitting a second pair of twins, by adapting the exclusion scene from *Amphitruo*, and by acknowledging the influence of the supernatural. We have also seen how, by reducing the dramatic function of fornication and adding a more serious dimension to the character of the Antipholus twins, he created something more complex and substantial, and at the same time made it possible to weave the Plautine farce into the now Christianized framework of the Greek romance. We must now consider how the whole process was assisted by Shakespeare's most original achievements – namely, the transformation of the nagging *matrona* into the many-sided and wholly human Adriana, and the creation of her different but equally credible sister.

To prepare the ground, we revert, for the last time, to St Paul and Ephesus. In his epistle to the Christian community in the city, which lays down the rules for godly marriage, Paul first of all condemns fornication: 'But fornication, and all uncleanness ... let it not be once named among you' (Ephesians 5.3); ... 'no whoremonger, nor unclean person ... hath any inheritance in the kingdom of Christ and of God' (Ephesians 5.5). Then, moving on to intramarital relations, Paul says, 'Wives, submit yourselves unto your own husbands, as unto the Lord. For the husband is the head of the wife, even as Christ is the head of the church' (22–3); 'Husbands, love your wives, even as Christ also loved the church, and gave himself for it' (25); 'Let every one of you ... so love his wife even as himself; and the wife see that she reverence her husband' (33).

With these precepts in mind, we return to *The Comedy of Errors*. At the opening of Act 2 it is two o'clock. Instead of starting dinner and letting Antipholus eat his cold when he arrives, Adriana has worked herself into a state, first, because her husband is free to wander wherever he pleases, whereas she must kick her heels at home. The second reason does not at once emerge, because Adriana and her sister energetically debate the first.

> *Luciana* Good sister let us dine and never fret;
> A man is master of his liberty. (2.1.6–7)
> ...
> *Adriana* Why should their liberty than ours be more?
> *Luciana* Because their business still lies out o' door (2.1.11)

(i.e., the husband's sphere is the city at large, the wife's is the home). As far as the working class was concerned, one doubts how far that division actually held good in London or Rome; but like Menaechmus, Antipholus is supposedly a respectable bourgeois; and so Luciana's acquiescence represents the conventional middle-class attitude. But Adriana rejects the convention. She retorts, in effect, 'when I treat *him* that way he doesn't like it.' Whereupon her sister irritates her still more by reminding her of the Pauline doctrine that husbands 'are masters of their families, and their lords' (24). 'Huh,' says Adriana, 'that's what prevents you from marrying; if you did marry, you'd insist on having some authority' (26, 28). But Luciana holds her ground: 'Ere I learn love I'll practise to obey' (29). This, of course, recalls the marriage-lines in *The Book of Common Prayer* (1549), where the bride promises to 'obey ... serve ... love ... honour and keep' her husband. And it is interesting to see (as one might have guessed) that already in Shakespeare's time the idea was not accepted everywhere without protest.

Luciana's words now prod Adriana into revealing the second reason for her disquiet.

How if your husband start some other where? (30)

Luciana again counsels patience:

Till he come home again I would forbear.

'All very well for you to recommend patience,' says Adriana, 'you've got nothing to be impatient about.' Dromio now enters. He was sent to fetch Antipholus, but failed to do so because, of course, he was speaking to the Syracusan, who gave him a smack on the ear. Adriana threatens to give him another, and sends him off again.[26] Luciana once more chides her for impatience (86), whereupon Adriana reveals that she is not only angry but miserable; and it's all because she thinks her husband is consorting with another woman. This moving speech is punctuated by Luciana, not with indignant remarks about Antipholus' alleged infidelity, but with reflections on the folly of jealousy (102, 116).

The theme of jealousy is resumed and developed in 2.2, where Adriana remonstrates with Antipholus in a way which shows that her distress arises from passionate affection allied to a rather pathetic sense of insecurity. In this most eloquent appeal she says, in effect, 'how would you like it if I were disloyal to you?'

How dearly would it touch thee to the quick,
Shouldst thou but hear I were licentious?
And that this body, consecrate to thee,
By ruffian lust should be contaminate?
Wouldst thou not spit at me, and spurn at me,
And hurl the name of husband in my face? (130–5)

All very moving, but, ironically, the appeal is addressed to the wrong man. More ironically still, the power of Adriana's appeal persuades the Syracusan to enter her house for dinner; and that leads directly to the pandemonium of the exclusion scene and the subsequent taunts of 'dissembling harlot' and 'unhappy strumpet' (4.4.99, 122).

We have already touched on the scene where the Syracusan pays court to Luciana (3.2). It begins when she makes a direct allusion to Ephesians 5.25 ('Husbands, love your wives' etc.):

> And may it be that you have quite forgot
> A husband's office? shall, Antipholus,
> Even in the spring of love, thy love-springs rot? (1–3)

Then a good-hearted attempt to combine realism with charity: are you really no longer in love with Adriana? Even if you married her for her money you might at least treat her with some decency. If you are carrying on with someone else, you ought to *pretend* that you're still fond of her and not hurt her feelings. But Antipholus continues to pour out his devotion and finally urges her to marry him. At this point Luciana quickly intervenes

> O soft, sir, hold you still;
> I'll fetch my sister to get her good will. (69–70)

I'm not sure what this means – perhaps no more than that Luciana will fetch her sister and tell her what has happened, so as to avoid putting herself in a false position. At any rate by 4.2 Luciana has reported the whole incident to Adriana. So much for her earlier contention that her sister should be kept in the dark. It looks as if secrecy was possible only as long as Antipholus was thought to be having an affair with just another woman; but once it appeared that Luciana herself was the object of his affections, then the matter could no longer be kept from her sister. In this later scene (4.2), Luciana perhaps reveals more than she intends; for it now becomes clear that she found Antipholus rather attractive, and was not just shocked, but also flattered, by his address:

Adriana With what persuasion did he tempt thy love?

Luciana With words that in an *honest* suit might move:
   First he did praise my beauty, then my speech.
Adriana (anxiously) Did'st speak him fair?
Luciana   Have patience, I beseech.
                  (13–16)

Patience again – and one notes that Luciana hasn't answered the question, though in fact she had said nothing to lead Antipholus on. This reticence provokes an explosion from Adriana:

He is deformed, crooked, old and sere,
Ill faced, worse bodied, shapeless everywhere;
Vicious, ungentle, foolish, blunt, unkind,
Stigmatical in making, worse in mind. (19–22)

Luciana (with feline softness):

Who would be jealous then of such a one?

Adriana recovers herself and admits the truth:

Ah but I think him better than I say.

So once again Adriana's jealousy is seen to arise from anxiety and overpossessiveness, not mere vindictiveness.

In the *Menaechmi*, when the *matrona* apprehends her (supposed) husband carrying the stolen dress, she sends for her father to come and deal with him (736). The old fellow knows that in matrimonial squabbles there are usually faults on both sides (765ff.), but he treats his daughter unsympathetically:

  Quotiens monstraui tibi, uiro ut morem geras,
 quid ille faciat, ne id obserues, quo eat, quid rerum gerat
               (788–9)[27]

How often have I told you to let your husband have his way, not to be spying on what he does, where he goes, and what he's up to?

This is a clumsy approach; for, whether the wife's nagging is the cause or the effect of Menaechmus' fornication, her father weighs straight in and directly alleges that she is at fault. The procedure of the abbess in 5.1 is altogether more subtle. In attempting to diagnose the source of Antipholus' disorder, she asks Adriana if it could be loss of money, or bereavement, or unlawful love. Adriana fastens on the last: 'some love that drew him oft from home' (56).

> Abbess   You should for that have reprehended him.
> Adriana   Why, so I did.
> Abbess   Ay, but not rough enough.
> Adriana   As roughly as my modesty would let me.
> Abbess   Haply in private.
> Adriana   And in assemblies too.
> Abbess   Ay, but not enough.
> Adriana   It was the copy of our conference;
>   In bed he slept not for my urging it,
>   At board he fed not for my urging it;
>   Alone, it was the subject of my theme;
>   In company I often glanc'd at it;
>   Still did I tell him it was vile and bad. (57–67)

And now the trap closes:

> Abbess   And thereof came it that the man was mad.

The abbess now goes through all the points confessed by Adriana, and concludes

> The consequence is, then, thy jealous fits
> Hath scar'd thy husband from the use of wits. (85–6)

All this is too much for Luciana. Although the abbess has said little more than what she herself said earlier ('Self-harming jealousy! fie, beat it hence' in 2.1.102; 'How many fond fools serve mad jealousy!' in 2.1.116), she is not prepared to hear her sister criticized by this strange woman. So she intervenes indignantly

She never reprehended him but mildly,
When he demean'd himself rough, rude, and wildly. (87–8)

Then, turning to Adriana,

Why bear you these rebukes and answer not?

Adriana (quietly)

She did betray me to mine own reproof (90)

– an interesting switch of emotional positions, in which Luciana becomes indignant and Adriana acquiescent. For the audience, the pleasure derived from this piece of moral enlightenment is only sharpened by the knowledge that the supposedly disordered male, who has given rise to it all, is the wrong man.

This clever psychological interplay takes us far from the Plautine comedy with which we began. Clearly the *Menaechmi* is altogether less complex and less serious. But before we say farewell to it we should acknowledge it for what it is. First, it is a work of great metrical virtuosity, consisting of speech (senarii), recitative (septenarii or octonarii chanted to a pipe) and song (various metres sung to the accompaniment of a pipe). Therefore, although the music is gone, and even professional Latinists are seldom at home with the lyric metres, one has to think of the *Menaechmi* as something akin to a musical comedy. This whole aspect of the work has been largely ignored in the present essay. Second, the *Menaechmi* is a skilful arrangement of comic scenes based on mistaken identity. No doubt some of the credit for this should go to the author of the Greek 'original.'[28] But we should beware of the prejudice which maintains that whatever is formally satisfactory in Plautus must come from his Greek model, while everything clumsy is Plautus' own. Along with the dramaturgical skill goes a certain homogeneity. Since, in dramatic terms, the *Menaechmi* does not pretend to be anything more than a heartless romp performed by two-dimensional comic types, it remains all of a piece. One has the impression that Plautus knew exactly what he was doing and did it well.

With Shakespeare, the case was different. As a young experimental dramatist, producing a new amalgam of comedy and romance, he could not be expected to attain formal perfection. An instance of imbalance may be seen in the treatment of the Syracusan Antipholus. As Luciana speaks to him in 3.2 he listens with increasing fascination. We cannot be sure how much he has taken in. Very little, perhaps, until she says

> Then, gentle brother, get you in again;
> Comfort my sister, cheer her, call her wife. (25–6)

'Gentle brother' – the phrase stuck when all else was perhaps a vague memory:

> And this fair gentlewoman, her sister here,
> Did call me brother. (5.1.373–4)

We have already heard how the Syracusan

> At eighteen years became inquisitive
> After his brother. (1.1.125–6)

He tells us as much himself in 1.2:

> So I, to find a mother and a brother,
> In quest of them, unhappy, lose myself. (39–40)

But now, long before he discovers his twin, here is someone who addresses him as 'brother,' and whom he greets as 'mine own self's better part' (3.2.61). Finally he says,

> Call thyself sister, sweet, for I am thee. (66)

The blend of souls is no less complete than when 'a drop of water ... seeks another drop' and falls 'to find his fellow forth' (1.2.35, 37). In the outcome, the discovery of Luciana as a soulmate detracts rather from the Syracusan's eventual meeting with his brother. Granted, Plautus drags out *his* recognition scene too long.

Between the moment when the astonished Messenio cries 'Good Lord! What do I see?' (1062) and the embrace of the two twins (1132) no fewer than seventy lines have elapsed. But Shakespeare surely goes too far in the other direction. At the climactic moment of their reunion the brothers do not exchange a single word. Almost as odd is the fact that Emilia addresses only three lines to her sons (5.1.400–2); and they do not speak to her at all. It must be added, however, that in an actual production there is so much going on (with Egeon, Emilia, Angelo, the Duke, two Antipholus twins, two Dromios, the two sisters, and others all on stage) that the anti-climax is barely noticed.

If we are emphasizing (as we must), not Shakespeare's deficiencies, but his amazingly original achievement in *The Comedy of Errors*, our last word must be about his characters. As we know, the characters of Shakespearian and Greek drama have gone through many vicissitudes in this century. They were turned loose from the text by A.C. Bradley and treated as real people; then rounded up and reincarcerated by L.C. Knights. They have been assimilated to the poet's language, as though they were a special kind of image or metaphor; treated as projections of the plot, or as fluid figures varying according to the rhetoric of the situation; more recently some critics have seen them as 'written' by the sociopolitical conditions of their day.

This is no moment to start a discussion of such ideas. But let us recall one point made earlier. While we know that Menaechmus frequently consorted with Erotium (358–72), we do not know how far his wife was to blame. Plautus leaves it open, and we assume he does so because the question is of no interest to him. Nor is it of any interest to us. In *The Comedy of Errors* the question of Antipholus' innocence remains unresolved. We were inclined to believe him when he told Balthasar that Adriana's accusations were unfounded (3.1.112). Yet later Luciana maintains that on more than one occasion 'he demean'd himself rough, rude, and wildly' (5.1.88). To dispose of this charge we have to assume that Luciana has been led by her indignant loyalty into making a baseless allegation. Now both these answers cannot be right. Both may be wrong, in the sense that Shakespeare himself may not have considered the question; perhaps he never envisaged or intended such speculation. But this much, I think, can be said. If I am wrong in raising this *kind* of problem, then countless readers over the last four centuries have been wrong too. And if such conjecture is misguided (as it may be, for the text does not provide the answer), it is just the kind of mistake that Shakespeare, throughout his *oeuvre*, encourages us to make. That beguiling spell is already at work in *The Comedy of Errors*.

CHAPTER THREE

Pope and Horace
Two Epistles
to Augustus

As with all imitations, Pope's *Epistle to Augustus* is based on the like and the unlike; and, as with the best of its kind, it possesses a double nature, being both a free-standing poem (English, eighteenth century, and Christian) and also an extended literary allusion, taking off from and returning to its Latin original. In this chapter, after illustrating the English / Roman parallel, I shall mention two opposing views of Augustus. I shall then describe not so much how Horace really felt about him as how he presented him in a given rhetorical context. The same procedure is followed in the case of Pope, with particular reference to Professor Weinbrot's revisionist thesis (1978). After that, I shall look at the ways in which Pope converted Horace's praise of Augustus into an attack on George II. Since neither epistle is wholly concerned with its addressee, something will be said about the confident classicism of the two poets in their treatment of earlier writing. I shall finish by calling attention to the manner in which Pope imported political and moral comment into passages where Horace had been purely literary, thus turning a Horatian epistle into a Popean satire.

As Erskine-Hill (1983) has shown, the period from 1680 to 1750 was not the first to claim the title of 'Augustan'; but that is now seen as the time when the parallels between England and Rome were at their most striking. If we compare, say, the London of 1750 with the Rome of 15 BC, we have two imperial capitals with a population of about three-quarters of a million. In each case growth had brought with it slums, overcrowding, filth, fire, and crime. The rich, naturally, liked to spend a fair proportion of their time in their villas, believing that a proper balance between town and country was essential to a civilized life. In Italy a lot of private building went on in the 20s – much to Horace's disapproval.[1] In England, too, after the South Sea Bubble, people hastened to invest in land, and a keen interest developed in country houses. Sumptuous books of designs began to appear, like Campbell's *Vitruvius Britannicus* (Vitruvius being, of course, a contemporary of Augustus). At the same time the grand tour enabled the well-to-do to inspect the Italian buildings for themselves. Burlington's visit in 1719 was especially important.

In that year Pope moved into his riverside house at Twickenham,[2] then a small village outside London. The three-storey house in five acres of ground offered considerable comfort, though it was an unpretentious place in comparison with the mansions of Bathurst, Ralph Allen, and Pope's other wealthy friends. So too Horace's place in the Sabine hills, though no palace, had eight servants, and five families lived off the estate. It was a place where the wilderness had been tamed by human effort, producing the kind of effect which Pope, in another context, described as 'nature methodiz'd.'

The two periods had much in common in their social stratigraphy, ranging from king and emperor, through the great landowners, the squires and wealthy merchants, to the common people, and from them down to the servants and slaves. To us both systems appear glaringly defective; yet the rich were not invariably callous. It was recognized that privileges entailed duties; and so one had obligations to one's dependants. That was the message of Cicero's *De Officiis*. The English read the same book, only they called it *Tully's Offices*; and they found that its teaching on good faith, patriotism, and social conduct could be reconciled well enough with the Christian gospel. Conversely, in the matter of religion, a deist hymn like Addison's 'The Spacious Firmament on High' (1712) or even Pope's own hymn beginning 'Father of all in every age / In every clime adored' would not have sounded outlandish to a Roman Stoic. Educated people in both ages regarded superstition as vulgar, and 'enthusiasm' as lacking in taste. But that kind of gentlemanly poise, it seems, can never be long maintained. By the 1740s John Wesley was lighting the flame of religious fervour in England; and just seventy years after Horace's death St Peter was crucified in Rome.

I turn now to the man who gave his name to both ages. I shall call him 'Octavian' in the years before he became emperor, and 'Augustus' thereafter. At the start of the *Annals*, Tacitus identifies two opposite views of his career. The first exonerated him of all blame for the dishonesty and violence that attended his rise to power: he was simply doing his duty to his dead father and yielding perforce to the pressures of the situation. The same view emphasized the peace and unity that characterized his regime, the restoration of legality, the moderate treatment of Rome's allies, and the adornment of the capital. The second view held that Octavian's 'dutifulness' and his pleas of reluctance were simply pretexts for his own single-minded lust for power. After Actium (31 BC) there was indeed peace, but peace stained with blood. The marriage laws of 18 BC brought ironical comments from those who remembered the adulterous seduction of Livia; and it was alleged that by setting up his own cult Augustus had left little room for the gods (*Annals* 1.9–10). In the eighteenth century, critics added the harsh measures of the emperor's last years, including the banishment of Ovid; and, like Tacitus, they insisted that the steps which Augustus took to mitigate his autocracy were, from the beginning, just different stages of a colossal confidence trick.

Now it takes little thought to see that, by themselves, both opinions are crude and simplistic. When Octavian entered on his inheritance, took Caesar's name, and vowed vengeance on Brutus and Cassius, he was acting *both* from filial piety *and* from personal ambition. The two motives reinforced each other. When he bribed the soldiers, outmanoeuvred Antony, and exploited Cicero, he was acknowledging the realities of revolutionary politics *as well as* satisfying his lust for power. Once he had entered the arena, there was no turning back. How could he have been expected to trust himself to the mercies of Antony? And when he heard that in Cicero's words 'the stripling was to be praised, honoured, and raised to heaven,' should he have dismissed the words as just another of the great man's witticisms?[3] This is not to deny that Octavian's role in the proscriptions is as deeply distasteful to us as it was to many at the time; nor is our distaste sweetened by the assurance that many of the victims escaped,[4] and that, as a rule, 'he who is strictly honest and unbending is not fit for the direction of public affairs.'[5] During the 30s Octavian was still very much the young revolutionary leader. Yet even then the features of the future emperor were discernible, just as the majestic face of the Prima Porta statue is foreshadowed by the early portrait from Pollentia, whose 'bony face, small eyes, and nervous expression ... seem truly to capture something of the ambitious and power-hungry young man.'[6] He was not without ideals. And when he achieved power he expressed in an edict his wish to be 'the founder of the best kind of state' – *optimi status auctor* (Suetonius, *Divus Augustus* 28.2). In realizing that dream he assumed, not without justice, that the interests of the city and empire coincided with his own.

One grants, of course, that Octavian played a major part in the destruction of the republic. But had he obeyed his mother and stepfather and avoided public life (Appian 3.2.10), would the system have survived? There can be only one answer. For all its achievements in earlier centuries, the senatorial aristocracy had shown itself incapable of holding together a large heterogeneous empire. The old class loyalties were too narrow and rigid. Nor could the state withstand the recurrent rivalries of ambitious generals. Eventually things reached a point where, it seems, there had to be a single authority. And it is clear that, except for a few disaffected senators (Suetonius 19), Augustus' authority was generally accepted. To hold him responsible for the crimes of his successors is a highly dubious procedure. The fact is that despite the worst excesses of later emperors Augustus' system lasted for four hundred years.

As for the charge that he elbowed out the gods, it would be truer to say that he *magnified* the gods in conjunction with himself and his family. The great temple of Mars Ultor, for example, was a monument to the founder of Rome, even though it also recalled the vengeance taken by Augustus on his father's murderers.[7] The emperor's personal cult was different in origin. He refused to be worshipped as a god in Rome in his own lifetime.

(Was he not princeps of a restored republic?) In Egypt and the Greek east, however, he was hailed spontaneously as a god, like Alexander and others before him. As a compromise he accepted that temples might be built to *Roma et Augustus* (in that order), and this procedure was extended to the west as well. In Italy practice varied. That is the situation described in Horace's epistle. It is true, however, that as time went on the line dividing association from assimilation became increasingly hard to draw.[8]

To finish this brief résumé, something must be said about the last five or six years of Augustus' regime, by which time Horace had been fifteen years dead. This was in many ways a dark and depressing period. The emperor was now over seventy. His program of moral reform had been defied by his daughter and granddaughter; his dynastic plans had gone tragically awry; the Pannonian revolt had been raging for over two years; there was a plague in Rome and famine in Italy. According to the elder Pliny (*Naturalis Historia* 7.149), these and other troubles brought Augustus to the verge of suicide. Such was the context in which Ovid made his fatal blunder – a blunder which must have had some political implications. Granted, the measure of liberty which had existed for thirty years was now being curtailed;[9] but Ovid was not a martyr in the cause of free speech. The part played in his ruin by the *Ars Amatoria*, though real enough, was subsidiary and retrospective.

Anyone who tries to draw up a balance sheet of Augustus' career *sine ira et studio* will probably find that when all account has been taken of the evils of the triumviral period, and all the negative features of the regime have been recorded, there is still a substantial credit balance in favour of the emperor. Even the unenthusiastic Tacitus, who belonged to the once all-powerful senatorial class, conceded that Augustus had the support of the people, that he was popular in the provinces, and that 'he won over the world by peace' (*Annals* 1.2). Likewise the modern Tacitus, Ronald Syme, ended his *Roman Revolution* by acknowledging that Augustus had 'saved and regenerated the Roman people'.[10]

In 30 BC, when the empire began, Horace was already thirty-five years old. He had published two books of *Satires* and a book of *Iambics*, or *Epodes*. Only in the very latest pieces did Octavian receive any serious recognition, even though Horace had belonged to his party by implication ever since joining Maecenas' circle in 37 BC. In the first collection of *Odes* (Books 1–3, published in 23 BC) Augustus was praised in only nineteen pieces out of eighty-eight.[11] True, most of these are important poems; yet the great majority of the odes (and many of the best loved) have nothing to do with politics. In Book 4, by which time Augustus was Horace's chief patron, the emperor with his family figured in six of the fifteen poems; but he had been ignored in the twenty epistles of Book 1 and the earliest epistle of Book 2 (viz. no. 2). This brought forth a mild remonstrance: 'Are you afraid,' said Augustus in a letter, 'that if you are seen to be a friend of mine it will blight your reputation with posterity?'[12] Horace therefore obliged with the *Epistle to Augustus*, but concluded his *oeuvre* (if we have the dates right) with the non-political *Ars Poetica*. So although Horace recognized Augustus' huge achievement, and was grateful for the way he had been treated by a former enemy, it is wrong to think of him primarily as a 'court poet.'

In some of the odes which do praise Augustus there are passages which we instinctively dislike. That does not absolve us from checking what Horace says or from using our historical imagination. In *Odes* 3.3, for instance, we are told that Augustus will eventually recline among the gods, drinking nectar with red lips. Doubtless at the time only the more naïve took the picture literally; but everyone accepted that in fact Augustus *would* be deified after his death. For sophisticated people this did not mean that the emperor was destined to be immortal, except in the sense that his fame would live on. And one of the things which guaranteed the survival of his fame was the fact that he had been praised by Horace: *caelo Musa beat*, 'the Muse confers the blessing of heaven' (*Odes* 4.8.29). In his greatest lyric (*Odes* 3.4) Horace speaks of his own childhood, which was watched over by the Muses. The Muses also watch over Augustus, refreshing him as he brings the civil wars to an end, and giving him 'gentle advice' (*lene consilium*). Here, instead of the poet being the mouthpiece of the Muses, they are the mouthpiece of the poet. The moral advice is repeated later with equal dexterity: 'power without wisdom crashes under its own weight' (*uis consili expers mole ruit sua*). In the first place, that is a comment on the fate of the Titans who tried to overthrow the Olympian gods. On another level it has clear reference to Antony. But Antony is now defeated and dead; and so the same profound truth is available for Augustus himself. That, to be sure, is flattery, but flattery with a humane and restraining purpose.

Our epistle, which has to do with poetry in the Roman state, opens with a comparison of Augustus' achievements to those of the gods and heroes of Greece and Rome. They, we are told, were not properly appreciated when on earth, but Augustus *is*:

> praesenti tibi maturos largimur honores
> iurandasque tuum per numen ponimus aras,
> nil oriturum alias, nil ortum tale fatentes (15–17)

> But you are honoured in good time while still among us.
> We build altars on which to swear by your divinity,
> declaring your like has never been and never will be.

That, we may feel, is laying it on a bit thick; but again Horace is only recording the facts. First, in Rome, Augustus *was* worshipped through his *genius* or *numen*. Second, it transpires that the Greek and Roman heroes are being used to introduce an essay on Greek and Roman poetry, in which poets are shown to be of value to the nation; in particular, *modern* poets are shown to be grossly neglected by the reading public. So once more the flattery has a tactical purpose: 'if the Romans can appreciate you in your lifetime, why can't they appreciate us?' But, whatever function we choose to dwell on, the tribute had to be selective. Horace himself could hardly bear to recall the disasters of the civil wars;[13] even in the 20s he must have been upset by the death of Gallus and by Augustus' harsh treatment of Maecenas. But there could be no question of adverse comment. So Horace ignored the emperor's bloody youth, and passed over his subsequent mistakes and misfortunes. Instead, he focused on his benign activities, stressing peace and defence, the laws which had transformed Rome's administration, the establishment of a great library, the support given to able writers. The resulting tribute does tell the truth – but not, of course, the whole truth. That was forbidden by the genre, and by the situation which gave rise to the poem.

Turning to the seventeenth and eighteenth centuries, we find a large range of opinions about Augustus – opinions gathered and discussed in the two brilliant books by Weinbrot (1978) and Erskine-Hill (1983). Many readers, I imagine, took up the former volume in the vague belief that Augustus, like Virgil and Horace, enjoyed general approval in Augustan England. Weinbrot will have changed that belief for good and all. But can it really have been, as his powerful exposition implies, that those who did approve of Augustus were just a rather unintelligent lot of time-serving royalists who soon became out of date, while the people who actually counted regarded Augustus as a tyrant and the two poets as his sycophants? At this point Erskine-Hill serves to restore the balance by arguing for a more complex mixture of views throughout the period. (It was possible, for instance, to admire Augustus' rule in general while deploring his rise to power.) The whole enormous question, as I shall argue presently, is peripheral to our enquiry; but a couple of points may be made. First, the detractors of Augustus talked a good deal about the destruction of freedom. Nowadays we would want to ask what freedom and whose? Were the provincials more, or less, free from exploitation under Augustus? Were traders more, or less, free from piracy? Were the *equites* more, or less, free to gain advancement in government service? Were the common people more, or less, free from famine and the danger of fire? Were all classes more, or less, free to intermarry? Was everyone more, or less, free from the fear of riot and civil war? In Pope's time such questions were rarely raised. Roman freedom meant largely the freedom of the senate. And people's views about this were naturally affected by their own view of the proper relation between king and parliament. So the freedom in question was that of the land-owning upper class, whether Roman or English.

A smaller, but related, question is that of flattery. As we know, flattery is endemic to all hierarchies, its intensity varying according to the rigidity of the system. In the two Augustan ages, no one would have addressed the monarch as an equal; an aristocrat, too, would expect to be approached with proper deference by an inferior. Pope's position was unusual. Having made a fortune from his translation of Homer, he could boast of being 'unplac'd, unpension'd, no Man's Heir or Slave.' Johnson, at the end of the age, was just able to survive without patronage, thanks to the development of periodicals. But in the main, flattery was taken for granted; it had to be conspicuously abject to excite disapproval. Consider, then, the following:

I have a privilege which is almost peculiar to myself; that I saw you in the east at your first rising above the hemisphere ... I was inspired to foretell you to mankind, as the restorer of poetry, the greatest genius, the truest judge, and the best patron ... It is your prerogative to forgive the many failings of those who ... cannot arrive to the heights that you possess from a happy, abundant, and native genius: which are as inborn to you as they were to Shakespeare.

That, believe it or not, is Dryden addressing the Earl of Dorset and Middlescx.[14] As I say, we must allow for convention. I only observe that the man who could grovel like that before a very minor figure was in no position to sneer at Horace for being 'a court slave.'

Bearing in mind, then, Horace's position, we should not see his epistle as a balanced appraisal, giving his full opinion of Augustus' strengths and weaknesses, but rather as a rhetorical construct, composed with a particular purpose in mind, in answer to a specific request. Or, to use the words of Pope's Advertisement, Horace 'paints [his Prince] with all the great and good qualities of a Monarch, upon whom the Romans depended for the Encrease of an *Absolute Empire*.' The portrait is idealized; and the traces of some highly unpleasant warts have been removed. But it is readily recognizable. Has Pope, then, taken the portrait at its face value, using it as a model for his own caricature of George II? Or has he, as Weinbrot would have us believe, tried to go behind it, criticizing the Roman as well as the English Augustus? (Saying, in other words, 'the Roman Augustus was awful, but ours is ten times worse.')

Leaving the epigraph,[15] we turn to Pope's Advertisement, or Preface. There he says 'to make the Poem entirely English, I was willing to add one or two of those Virtues which contribute to the Happiness of a *Free People*, and are more consistent with the Welfare of *our Neighbours*.' The 'Virtues' are ostensibly associated with George II, but the irony is unmistakable. The king and Walpole were under constant attack from the opposition on the grounds that the government's corruption was undermining English liberty.[16] In 1737 (the year of the epistle's publication) the introduction of stage censorship was highly topical and controversial. And, in Pope's view perhaps worst of all, Roman Catholics were still 'Deny'd all Posts of Profit or of Trust' (*Epist.* 2.2.61). As for 'the Welfare of *our Neighbours*,' that is best taken as referring to lines 221-8, where Pope honours the courageous resistance of Swift to England's oppression of Ireland. So far, the Advertisement, while not incompatible with Weinbrot's theory, does not establish it. The same applies to the central paragraph.[17] The concluding passage says, 'Horace made his Court to this Great Prince, by writing with a decent freedom toward him, with a just Contempt of his low Flatterers, and with a manly regard to his own Character.' The decent freedom is seen in the relaxed and confident tone in which Horace criticizes contemporary taste – criticisms acknowledged by Pope in the central paragraph of the Advertisement; the flatterers are dismissed in Horace's comic conclusion (260–70); and Horace's self-respect is seen in the forthright defence of his profession. (It is easy to forget that the emperor of the Roman world is being lectured on his cultural policy by the son of a former slave.) So there is no reason to suspect irony here. And there is some advantage in reading the passage straight; for then not only can the Great Prince be contrasted with George II, but Horace's 'decent freedom,' 'just contempt,' and 'manly regard' can be taken as an assertion about Pope's epistle too.

The actual text of Pope's epistle, as far as I can see, provides no firm basis for an answer to our question. So are there any external arguments available? Four possibilities suggest themselves.

1 / While agreeing with Weinbrot that 'from the beginning of his

career as an imitator Pope had felt free to change and transcend his parent-poem' (183), I cannot find any other case where the parent poem has been turned on its head. But, you say, is that not what Pope has done? In fact, no. He has left Horace's favourable portrait of Augustus unaltered, but has set beside it a caricature of George II, with the same pose and the same imperial trappings.

2 / If the revisionists' theory were correct, one would expect to find such an important insight at least referred to by the editors closest to Pope in time. Yet there is no trace of the idea in Warburton; and Warton knows nothing of it. In his edition the latter quotes Pope's words about Horace's 'decent freedom' and his 'contempt for low flatterers.' He then adds that Pope 'surely forgot the 15th and 16th lines' – i.e., the lines about the semi-divine honours paid to Augustus. In other words, Warton thought Pope had been somewhat careless, but he did not detect any irony.

3 / In a letter to Dr Arbuthnot, written a couple of years before, Pope says, 'It was under the greatest Princes and the best Ministers that moral satyrists were most encouraged' (Sherburn 1956, 3.420). He then goes on to contrast the friendly attitude of Augustus with the hostility of Nero and Domitian. Once again, Pope's considered view of Augustus (whatever its mixture of admiration and disapproval) is not in point. Like the epistle, the letter shows how Pope could *use* the emperor in a specific context, without irony, as an exemplar of the enlightened ruler.

4 / If George Augustus is to be seen as an extension or intensification of Caesar Augustus rather than as a disastrous contrast, the force and clarity of the satire are greatly weakened. Black on white is sharper than black on grey.[18] For these reasons it seems best to assume that Pope's satirical stance is the same as Johnson's in the latter's epigram:

Augustus still survives in Maro's Strain,
And Spenser's Verse prolongs Eliza's Reign;
Great George's Acts let tuneful Cibber sing;
For Nature form'd the Poet for the King.

Given this attitude, how did Pope convert the honorific sections of Horace's epistle into an anti-royalist satire? At the beginning, Horace recalls how Romulus, Bacchus, and Hercules served mankind, yet failed to earn adequate appreciation when on earth. Augustus, however, who has performed similar feats, is honoured in his *lifetime*. Pope's opening, though more hyperbolical, represents a plausible imitation. It is only when the lines are applied to George Augustus instead of Caesar Augustus that they are transformed into a piece of insolent mockery:[19]

> While You, great Patron of Mankind, sustain
> The balanc'd World, and open all the Main;
> Your Country, chief, in Arms abroad defend,
> At home, with Morals, Arts, and Laws amend.

The last monarch whom Pope called 'Patron of Mankind' was the great Marcus Aurelius (*Temple of Fame*, 167), who not only ruled over a huge empire but also, as a Stoic, believed in the unity of mankind. 'Sustain the balanc'd World' was taken from a poem of Lyttleton's, where it referred to Godolphin's maintenance of the balance of power.[20] But the phrase owes its pomposity (one suspects) to the image of Atlas with the globe on his shoulders. 'Open all the Main' now switches its meaning from 'clear the sea for British trade' to 'leave the sea open to Spanish pirates.'[21] 'In Arms abroad' reminds the eighteenth-century reader that the king has just spent eight months abroad in the arms of Mme de Wallmoden. In line 4 'Arts' stands out because it is not in Horace. As was well known, George II ignored the arts, except for music. All in all, the opening of a virtuoso. In 7ff. Pope now substitutes Edward III, Henry V, and King Alfred for Horace's deified heroes. The claim is that George Augustus has equalled their achievements and surpassed them in good fortune; for his stature, allegedly unlike theirs, is recognized while he is still alive. The actual contrast is not only ludicrous, but also deeply damaging to the present king, in that Edward, Henry, and Alfred had all been annexed by the opposition as icons of English greatness, both as conquerors and as champions of liberty.[22]

Much later (350) Pope again addresses the king, urging him to extend his patronage to non-dramatic poets:

> Or who shall wander where the Muses sing?
> Who climb their mountain, or who taste their Spring?
> How shall we fill a Library with Wit,
> When Merlin's Cave is half unfinish'd yet?

By the time of Pope's epistle, Merlin (the magician and prophet connected with the Brutus legend and King Arthur) had been used in Hanoverian propaganda by authors like Theobald, Jacob and Dryden – the implication being that George II was an Arthur *rediuiuus*.[23] So we would expect any reference to Merlin by Pope to be critical. And that is indeed the case here. Merlin's Cave at Richmond was a house which, it was proposed, would contain a choice collection of English books. It was a smallish building with a thatched roof, and Pope remarks with some disdain that it could not really be called a *library*. Yet even that gesture towards literature was not made by the king; it was Queen Caroline's idea. By using it to point a ridiculous contrast to the great Greek and Latin library on the Palatine, Pope showed his usual alertness and opportunism. He then continues:

> My Liege! why Writers little claim your thought,
> I guess;

the pause leaves a split second for the real reason to suggest itself (i.e., 'because you are a stupid philistine'); then at once, on behalf of his colleagues, Pope takes the blame: poets are tactless and tiresome people, who write epistles to the king and expect the kind of recognition that Louis XIV lent to Boileau and Racine. (How absurd to hope for anything like that from you!) Even if the monarch is too busy to choose his own encomiast, he should appoint some minister

> Fit to bestow the Laureat's weighty place (379),

which means that Walpole, who had appointed Cibber to that post, was patently *unfit*. And so was Cibber; for if we glance across at the Latin we find the corresponding phrase printed in Roman characters: INDIGNO POETAE. Here, as in other places, an unworthy laureate reflects the decline of the monarchy.

After thirty lines of such raillery Pope prepares a more deadly thrust (380ff.). Charles I and William III, like Alexander long ago, had taken care to employ the very best portrait painters, but had shown no discernment in poetry. We wait to see how George Augustus is going to be distinguished from those injudicious kings. Horace had been quite explicit:

> Your own judgement of poets, however, is fully upheld
> by your favourite writers Virgil and Varius; also the presents
> they have received reflect the greatest credit on you. (245–7)

How, then, will Pope adapt these lines? His answer is to print them in Roman, to enclose them in brackets, and to leave an accusing gap. There is no conceivable counterpart to Virgil, no parallel to a generous princeps.

Then come a dozen lines of mock celebration (390ff.), recording the non-feats which Pope would *like* to honour – triumphs of appeasement and sloth in which the nod is not that of authority but that of somnolence:

> when you nodded, o'er the land and deep,
> Peace stole her wing, and wrapt the world in sleep.[24]

The epistle ends with a clever piece of *aemulatio*, in which Pope rethinks Horace's comic conclusion. 'I am unable,' says Horace, 'to supply a fit encomium, and Your Majesty will not accept anything paltry. Caution is needed in such matters. A ridiculous failure is better remembered (such is human malice) than a serious act of homage.' Then, to spare the emperor's dignity, Horace himself takes the place of the great man who hates the idea of being celebrated by an incompetent:

> I fear I'd flush on receiving so coarse a tribute; in no time
> I'd be laid in a closed box beside my poetic admirer,
> then carried down to the street that deals in perfume
> and incense and pepper and anything else that's wrapped in useless
> pages.

Instead of playing the recipient, Pope poses as the writer of the vile encomium (405ff.). He is the fool who is so maladroit that when he aims to praise he seems fated to wound. The praise he has just uttered, he pretends, is sincere; if it appears offensive, that is quite unintentional. But to be on the safe side he will not attempt a full-dress eulogy. Such poems, when written by fools like himself, demean the subject if they are factually true, and libel him if they are not; for

Praise undeserv'd is scandal in disguise.

When that maxim is applied to the adulation lavished on the king in 395–403, little is left standing of George's reputation. If Pope ever does produce such rubbish, he adds, may it join the panegyrics by Eusden, Philips, and Settle, and be used as waste paper, or left to flutter on the railings of Bedlam.

Pope's satirical jibes naturally make his epistle sharper and more entertaining than the original. Consequently what we miss in Pope is the impression of poet and ruler collaborating in the same great enterprise. According to Suetonius, Augustus 'encouraged the talents of his own age in every way. He listened with courtesy and patience to people reciting – not just poems and histories, but speeches and dialogues too' (89.3). So in addressing Augustus Horace is probably not urging him to direct his attention to an area previously ignored, as Pope inferred, but rather encouraging him to continue (perhaps more energetically) what he was doing already, just as he urged him to continue stocking the Palatine library (216–18).

I turn now to what might be called the problem of classical theory. Roman literature, as everyone knows, developed under the influence of Greece (Horace, *Epistulae* 2.156–7). But to Horace, looking back two hundred years from an age of high urban culture, the early pioneers of Roman epic and drama seemed artistically uncouth. For all their energy, they marked only the beginning of a process which was still not quite complete: 'even today,' says Horace (160), 'there are traces of our rustic past.' Much earlier, in third-century Greece, Xenocrates had discerned an analogous evolution in sculpture and painting. His perceptions (which can be partly reconstructed from chapters in the elder Pliny) were introduced to Italy by Varro;[25] and it may have been Varro on whom Cicero was drawing when he compared Livius' version of the *Odyssey* to a statue by Daedalus, and Naevius' *Punic War* to a work of Myron's.

According to Cicero, the development of sculpture from Canachus and Calamis, through Myron to Polycleitus, had also a parallel in Roman oratory, which started with Cethegus, continued with Cato, and had now (one infers) reached its high point with Cicero himself. It had all been a natural progression; for nothing reaches perfection at the time of its discovery: *nihil est enim simul et inuentum et perfectum* (*Brutus* 71). This evolutionary approach, which was continued by Quintilian (12.10.1-9), was resumed at the time of the renaissance (e.g., in the work of Vasari), and is still familiar today. Thus, in her history of Greek art, Gisela Richter shows how, for instance, in the kouros type, sculptors gradually discovered 'the true nature of appearance.' Among the chief signposts are 'Cleobis and Biton,' the 'Critios Boy,' the 'Doryphoros' of Polycleitus, the 'Apollo Sauroctonos' of Praxiteles, and then, at the end of the road, the 'Apoxyomenos' of Lysippus.[26] Similarly, in his chapter on the Florentines in *Italian Painting of the Renaissance*, Bernard Berenson takes us from Giotto and Masaccio through various intermediaries to Michelangelo, in whom 'Florentine art had its logical culmination.'[27]

Towards the end of his epistle Horace speaks of Alexander, who insisted on being painted by Apelles and modelled by Lysippus (each of whom was often regarded as representing the high point of his medium), but was unwise enough to pay the wretched Choerilus to celebrate him in verse (232–45). What Horace does not bring out is that, since Greek epic had reached its acme long ago with Homer, Alexander could not have called on the preeminent exponent of the genre. By contrast Augustus, for complex historical reasons and in a complex way, was associated with Virgil, whose work represented the acme of *Latin* epic. On the other hand, although there were some highly expert sculptors working at the time (witness the Prima Porta statue and the figures on the *Ara Pacis*), they could not have enjoyed more than

a 'neo-classical' status. Anyhow, as Greeks, they were not acknowledged as part of Rome's patriotic tradition. Horace does not
name them, any more than he names the poet Crinagoras.

Let us look a little more closely at the evolutionary idea, confining ourselves to Latin poetry. How fruitful is it? In epic we
have, first, Greek material in Italian form (Livius' *Odyssey* in
Saturnians), then Italian material in Italian form (Naevius' *Punic
War*), and finally Italian material in Greek form (Ennius' *Annals*
in hexameters). So, in Aristotelian terms, Latin epic might be said
to have reached its formal *telos* with Ennius. But of course that
takes no account of subsequent *stylistic* developments. Unfortunately, almost no epic has survived from the period between
Ennius and Virgil. (To obtain evidence we have to bend the rules
and make use of Lucretius.) Yet there is still every justification
for seeing the *Aeneid* as the culmination of the whole process.
Silver epic marks a decline. In tragedy, Roman critics had detected individual virtues in Ennius, Pacuvius and Accius (*Epistles*
2.1.158–67). But rather than commenting on their respective
merits Horace was concerned to establish that as a whole early
writers were crude. They had energy and power, but were unwilling to take the requisite care (*Epistles* 2.1.165–6; *Ars Poetica* 258-
62, 290–1). Presumably an Augustan exemplar would have been
Varius' *Thyestes*, of which Quintilian thought quite highly
(10.1.98). But in any case Horace, in his rather sketchy remarks,
ignores the question of development and operates only with
'early' versus 'modern.' The same is true of his survey of comedy.
Leaving out Livius, Naevius, and Ennius, he begins with Plautus,
criticizing him for lack of subtlety in his characters and for his
slipshod construction; all he cares about is his fee (*Epistles*
2.1.170–6). No improvement is noted in the Italian comedies of
Afranius (*Ars Poetica* 288–91), who wrote in the late second
century, or even in those of Atta, who lived until 77 BC (*Epistles*
2.1.79ff.). Again, because he is protesting at conservative prejudice, Horace implies that everything written before his time was
crude and slovenly. But what about Terence? He had died over a
century earlier; yet Horace must have realized that in stylistic
finish he marked a notable advance on Plautus; in fact, Horace
adapted a scene of Terence in one of his own satires.[28]

Nothing is said in the epistle about satire, probably because it was not an 'official' genre; and anyhow it had already been handled in *Satires* 1.10. Even there, however, the development of the form receives a very cursory treatment. Lucilius was the inventor; Varro of Atax and certain others had attempted it without success (*Satires* 1.10.48, 46–7). So we are left with just two exponents, one at the beginning of the tradition (Lucilius) and the other (Horace himself) marking the culmination. By studying Lucilius' fragments we can get some idea of what Horace meant when he complained that his predecessor was harsh in his versification, overly keen on Greek expressions, too sharp in his attacks, too broad in his humour, and generally muddy and verbose.[29] If, then, Horace is accepted as the classical exponent of satire, it is not hard to see Persius (for all his distinctive qualities) as marking a decline. But in that case what are we to make of Juvenal? By some of the classical criteria he fails; but his stature is so strongly attested by other features that to talk of 'decline' is out of place. He takes the decadent hyperbole of silver Latin, and turns it to his own advantage by using it as a vehicle of wit. So much for satire. As for pastoral and lyric, they were not imported until the end of the republic, and so there was no possibility of development. Virgil's *Eclogues* and Horace's *Odes* were both the earliest instances and the best.

So the evolutionary theory is not uniformly helpful, and when the classical idea is equated with the highest excellence it can lead to unfairness. Proportion, economy, elegance, euphony – these, to be sure, are positive virtues; but they are not the *only* virtues. If the best contemporary drama surpassed the older works in artistry, did it equal them in power? If we possessed a sufficient sample we might well have doubts. Did Fundanius, for instance, combine Plautus' vigour with the elegance of Terence? In satire Horace himself seldom rivalled, in fact seldom *tried* to rival, Lucilius in the trenchancy of his attacks. Again, are there not some passages of Lucretius where a certain cragginess is appropriate to the subject, where the reader should have to *work* a bit to meet the poet? All that seems plain enough. But then the other horn of the dilemma confronts us. For if we always set out to meet Lucretius (or anyone else) solely on his own terms, we may find ourselves without a *point d'appui* when we want to voice a reservation. Older readers will recall that Kitto did much for Aeschylus by refusing to assess him by Sophoclean standards. At the same time, Kitto's method seemed to deprive him of a basis for expressing any misgivings at all. The problem arises again when the classical moment has gone by. One sympathizes with a poet like Lucan as he tries to cope with 'the burden of the past'; it is only right to ask what he is trying to do and why. Yet in the end one must retain the right to say that in all major respects his work is on a lower level than Virgil's. Otherwise one becomes lost in a fog of relativism.

Such are the problems inherent in the classical stance so confidently adopted by Horace. Pope's confidence was no less. In his epistle he followed Horace in omitting any reference to satire. But we can see the kind of standards which he had in mind if we look at the poems entitled *The Satires of Dr. John Donne, Dean of St. Paul's, Versified* – as if Dr Donne had written them in prose. Like Dryden before him,[30] Pope compared Donne to Lucilius, as he showed by prefixing the following lines to his versions:

Quid uetat, et nosmet Lucili scripta legentes
Quaerere, num illius, num rerum dura negarit
Versiculos natura magis factos, et euntes
Mollius? (*Satires* 1.10.56–9)

So why shouldn't *we* inquire as we read Lucilius' writings
whether it was his own harsh nature or that of his times
which prevented his verse from being more finished and
smoothly flowing?

This implied that Pope admired Donne, but considered his style rather primitive. What did he mean and what kind of changes did he desire? Here is a very brief excerpt from the beginning of Donne's fourth satire (probably written in 1579). Donne meets an exceedingly tiresome character when on his way to court:

Well; I may now receive, and die; My sinne

Indeed is great, but I have beene in
A Purgatorie, such as fear'd hell is
A recreation to, and scarse map of this.
My minde, neither with prides itch, nor yet hath been
Poyson'd with love to see, or to bee seene,
I had no suit there, nor new suite to shew,
Yet went to Court.

This is Grierson's text (except that he prints the long s). In l.1 'receive' means 'receive holy communion.' The metre of l.2 is lame, and the reading 'but yet I have beene in' appears in later versions. In ll.3–4 Grierson (followed by Milgate and Carey) has improved the construction by restoring 'to' after 'recreation' (i.e., 'in comparison to which hell is a recreation'). But Pope seems not to have had that reading. 'Scarse,' though defended by Grierson, is abandoned by more recent editors in favour of 'scant.' Lines 5–6 give an intelligible, if rather involved, construction: 'my mind hath been poisoned neither with pride's itch nor with love to see or to be seen.' (The reading 'yet hath seen' is one of the Twickenham edition's all too numerous mistakes.) The rhythm, which involves scanning 'neither' as a pyrrhic (i.e., with two light syllables) is harsh, and one notes the later variant 'nor.' But again 'neither' seems to have been what Pope read. Finally, in l.7 we have a pun on 'suit.' Taste in puns is notoriously subjective. Donne clearly thought this one was good enough; Pope didn't. Here, then, is Pope's rewriting of the lines:

Well, if it be my time to quit the Stage,
Adieu to all the Follies of the Age!
I die in charity with Fool and Knave,
Secure of Peace at least beyond the Grave.
I've had my *Purgatory* here betimes,
And paid for all my Satires, all my Rhymes:
The Poet's Hell, its Tortures, Fiends and Flames,
To this were Trifles, Toys, and empty Names.
      With foolish *Pride* my heart was never fir'd,
Nor the vain Itch *t'admire*, or *be admir'd*;
I hop'd for no *Commission* from his Grace;

I bought no *Benefice*, I begg'd no *Place*;
Had no *new Verses*, or *new Suit* to show;
Yet went to Court!

The clarity of thought, the regular rhythm, the end-stopped lines, the elaboration of the wit (which still remains specific), the characteristic (and deceptive) ease – all betoken the classical sensibility and technique. Yet, if the Satires have been 'versified,' they are no longer anything like the Satires of Dr Donne. To take up the historical point, Pope may well have thought that, since Donne, there had been progress in satirical writing; that Dryden, for instance, possessed the vigour of Donne plus a modern classical style. But that is not how he weights the argument in his epistle. Here, like Horace, he says little about progress, and works instead with the broad categories 'old' (i.e., pre-Pope) and 'modern' (Pope). Thus

E'en copious Dryden wanted, or forgot,
The last and greatest Art, the Art to blot. (280–1)

If Pope admired Donne, he revered Shakespeare. Others, of course, did so too. Earlier in the century Rowe had praised Shakespeare's natural gifts, and refused to judge his plays by the rules of Aristotle. Dennis pointed to his originality, his lifelike characters, and his power over the passions. Unlike Rowe, however, he regretted his deficiencies in scholarship and his lack of art. He disapproved of the rabble in *Julius Caesar*; and, like Johnson later, he was disturbed by Shakespeare's lack of 'Poetic Justice.' To mitigate Shakespeare's stylistic shortcomings Dennis invoked the scanty time available to a busy actor. After Pope, Theobald said, 'Shakespeare's Clinches, false Wit, and descending beneath himself may have proceeded from a Deference paid to the then reigning Barbarism.' All these opinions are found, more vividly expressed, in Pope.[31] But only Pope carried his principles to such drastic lengths in shaping his text. In this he behaved like a neo-classical Procrustes, thinking, as Johnson said, 'more of amputation than of cure.' Pope, in fact, was not equipped to deal with the difficulties of a Shakespearian editor's task – the chaotic spelling and punctuation, the occasional meaningless word, the discrepancies between quarto and folio, the changes that had taken place in English forms and grammar.[32]

Undignified matter posed another problem. In many cases Pope simply pronounced the offending passages spurious and consigned them to the bottom of the page. A small example is Cassius' line 'Now is it Rome indeed and room enough' (*Julius Caesar* 1.2.155). Disliking the play on words, Pope 'degraded' this and the next line. In *The Tempest* 2.1.9ff, after the beginning of Alonso's speech 'Prythee peace,' Pope says 'all that follows ... seems to have been interpolated (perhaps by the players) ... not only being very impertinent stuff, but most improper and ill-placed drollery in the mouths of unhappy shipwrecked people.'[33] Other unsatisfactory passages, however, are retained with the excuse that Shakespeare had 'to please the populace.' Hence, in tragedy, strange events and bombastic diction; in comedy, 'mean buffoonery, vile ribaldry, and unmannerly jests of fools and clowns.' To balance all this censure, Pope printed commas opposite lines which he particularly admired, and stars at the beginning of favourite scenes. From the handful of plays I have inspected no clear pattern emerges; John Butt, however, from a much larger sample, concluded that Pope was especially drawn to descriptive and sententious passages, often signalling his approval of non-dramatic 'messenger-work' and the expression of universal truths (1936, 6–16).

Pope's Shakespeare, then, like a gastronomic guide, is mainly of interest as an index of the editor's taste. As a piece of monstrously misguided scholarship it seems to me to come second only to Bentley's Milton. And that raises another thought which is so uncomfortable that I prefer to put it as a question: since virtually all the principles of Bentley and Pope are enunciated by Horace, can it be that he is responsible, at least in part, for those two notorious editions?

Though Horace enters a number of vivid and amusing complaints about the conservatism of the reading public and the vulgarity of theatre audiences, we do not know whose case he is pleading, apart from that of Virgil, Varius, and himself. (Did he also have in mind Fundanius and Pollio, for instance?) How widespread was the alleged indifference to the new classicism? And what was its basis? More information is available in the case of Pope. We know he was subjected to all kinds of personal abuse based on his physique, his class, his religion, and his politics – abuse more savage than any experienced by Horace.[34] His parodies and imitations were criticized uncomprehendingly for plagiarism and inaccuracy; his expressions were analysed (often unfairly) with a pedantic literalism; even his versification was condemned for monotony. Yet it is still not clear how general such stylistic criticism was; nor can we tell from the epistle how far (if at all) Pope is championing a group of modern poets. In the main he seems to be speaking for himself.

What is clear is that Pope thought Horace's judgments on poetry past and contemporary were 'seasonable to the present times.' He therefore adopted Horace's polemical stance, which determined the thrust and direction of his argument. This entailed a problem; for all his Augustan confidence, Pope was fully aware of the gigantic stature of Chaucer, Shakespeare, Milton, and Dryden. Yet the rhetoric of the situation obliged him to point up their shortcomings; thus Shakespeare achieved immortality in spite of himself (72); Milton's stylistic level was uneven (99–100); Dryden failed to revise his work (281). Now when we take all Horace's statements into account, we conclude that he too found much to admire in the early poets (especially Ennius and Lucilius).[35] And he had sufficient historical sense to realize that their way of writing went with their period. (He may possibly have thought that a major archaic poet possessed, as it were, a certain ratio of *ars* to *ingenium*, and that if the proportion of *ars* were increased to meet Augustan standards, the proportion of *ingenium* would diminish. Or did he think that all the Augustan poets were to a greater or lesser extent like Virgil, whose craftsmanship actually enhanced his power? We can only speculate.) But in the epistle, because of his polemical stance, Horace projects an attitude of superiority. Pope is somewhat more circumspect. He alludes to Shakespeare's merits (72, 119), and those of Milton (99) and Dryden (267–9); and he acknowledges 'that greater faults than we / They had, and greater Virtues' (95–6). On the other hand, he broadens Horace's criticism (which is confined to

matters of craftsmanship) in ways which I shall mention presently.

Before going any further, however, I should like to point to one
passage which Pope transferred from the Latin almost holus
bolus, viz. ll.49–68, based on Horace 34–49. Pope, it will be observed, has taken twenty lines to Horace's sixteen; but then he is
working with a line of ten syllables, whereas Horace's hexameter
has an average of fourteen or fifteen. And Pope has the added task
of finding rhymes. That said, it is hard to know what to admire
most. In the first ten verses pure iambics are interspersed with
variations – inversions (i.e., trochee for iambus) in the first foot
(50 and 51), a spondee in the first (53) and in the second (56),
inversion in the fourth (57). Pauses occur after the first and third
feet (51), after the first and second (52), after the second (53), after
the third (57), in the middle of the fourth (56 and 58). Such subtle
changes of pace become apparent when the passage is read aloud.
The rhymes, as ever, seem totally natural. Presumably 'a heap of
snow' was devised to go with the old chronicler Stowe; but the
trick is performed with such ease that we are hardly aware of it.
And what a graphic substitution for *Libitina sacrauit*: 'Bestow a
garland only on a Bier' (68)! The closely reasoned dialogue sounds
as spontaneous as Horace's own; and our attention is arrested by
the happy collocation of 'Wit' and 'Wine,' the intransitive use of
'immortalize,' the occurrence of 'Classick' as a noun, and the
clever adaptation of the legal phrase 'By courtesy of England.' All
that, and more, is going on in a passage where Pope has largely
refrained from introducing new material:

> If Time improve our Wit as well as Wine,
> Say at what age a Poet grows divine?
> Shall we, or shall we not, account him so,
> Who dy'd, perhaps, an hundred years ago?
> End all dispute; and fix the year precise
> When British bards begin t'Immortalize?
> 'Who lasts a Century can have no flaw,
> 'I hold that Wit a Classick, good in law.
>   Suppose he wants a year, will you compound?
> And shall we deem him Ancient, right and sound,

Or damn to all Eternity at once,
At ninety nine, a Modern, and a Dunce?
'We shall not quarrel for a year or two;
'By Courtesy of England, he may do.
     Then, by the rule that made the Horse-tail bare,
I pluck out year by year, as hair by hair,
And melt down Ancients like a heap of snow:
While you, to measure merits, look in Stowe,
And estimating Authors by the year,
Bestow a Garland only on a Bier.

In sketching his history of Roman drama Horace draws several (sometimes artificial) parallels with Greece. Over and above that, he uses Greece / Rome as a kind of leitmotif which serves to connect the courtly framework with the main (literary) body of the epistle. Thus the native Romulus is named with Greek heroes (5); Augustus excels Greek and Roman leaders (19); the earliest Greek poetry, unlike the earliest Latin, was the best (28ff.); Latin writers are compared with Greek predecessors (50, 57–8); Roman conservatism is contrasted with Greek love of novelty (90–117); Augustus, unlike Alexander, is a discerning literary critic (232–47). This continuous comparison was not available to Pope, who moved from Greece and Rome (20, 43) to France (145, 263, 274ff., 375). The French dimension did not satisfy Warton, who thought Pope should have acknowledged the influence of Italy. Others have pointed out that the rise of satire, as described by Pope (241ff.), has no historical basis. There are also other, less significant, anomalies.[36] But these are not the passages that make Pope's epistle memorable.

Far more important are the sections which have to do with writing in London, not least writing for the stage. Pope knew a fair number of actors and actresses, and took a lively interest in the theatre. He collaborated with Gay and Arbuthnot in *Three Hours after Marriage*, and wrote the Prologue to Cibber's *The Provoked Wife*. Nor, in spite of what he implies about the superiority of new to old, did he underrate earlier work. He had a high opinion, for instance, of Ben Jonson's *The Silent Woman*, which was often played in the eighteenth century. In tragedy he quite admired Webster and Marston, and thought well of Dryden's *All for Love*. In his own day he advised Addison, Sheffield, and a dozen others about the style and composition of their plays. Yet in one respect he was in a rather difficult position; for while he believed that tragedy must have pathos, he was suspicious of high-flown turgid language, and he deprecated a pompous and monotonous delivery.[37] (Thus he enjoyed Gay's parody of tragic emotion in *The What D'Ye Call It*, and may even have contributed to that work.) Why, then, did he find so many tragedies acceptable? It was largely, in Goldstein's view (1958, 116), because of the importance he attached to moral and didactic writing. (One recalls those shining passages in Shakespeare to which he drew attention.) Perhaps, too, more mischievously, he approved of a genre which could be given a topical interpretation, as when the tyrannical villain of the piece could be identified with Walpole. For whatever reason, Pope was personally involved in the legitimate theatre. Part of his dislike of Theobald, Settle, Rich and Cibber stemmed from their promotion of the pantomime – a genre which had even less intellectual content than Italian opera, with its warbling eunuchs. In voicing such views Pope stood at least on the fringe of the theatrical profession, whereas Horace spoke only as a spectator.

It goes without saying that London writing was part of London life. The epistle gives us the names of playwrights, actors, hymn-writers, doctors, painters, an architect, and a money-lender; titles of plays and a popular tune; the names of a pub,[38] a miniature library, and an asylum. The race course at Newmarket is a playground for the London rich, and even that wild romantic couplet

> Loud as the Wolves, on Orcas' stormy Steep,
> Howl to the roarings of the Northern Deep (328–9)

has, as its *raison d'être*, the description of a London theatre audience. In this cavalcade of city life, as one snapshot follows another, we become aware that for Pope those few square miles on the Thames represent the centre of the world. Foreign influences, like French romances and Italian opera, are treated with a quite un-Horatian contempt. And yet, at the same time, those metropolitan ceremonies, still so beloved of the English, are mocked in a spirit which is a good deal less affectionate than that of W.S. Gilbert:

> Pageants on pageants, in long order drawn,
> Peers, Heralds, Bishops, Ermin, Gold and Lawn;
> The Champion too! and to complete the jest,
> Old Edward's Armour beams on Cibber's breast! (316–19)

The coronation of Henry VIII and Anne Boleyn was presented as part of Shakespeare's play in 1727, but was staged on a number of other occasions in the same year. The actor playing the Champion wore the armour of Edward III, borrowed from the Tower of London – a woeful breach of decorum.[39]

While the Church of England escapes ridicule, allusions to Christianity occur in contexts of satire. For instance, the words of the Nicene Creed ('I look for the resurrection of the dead and the life of the world to come') form part of a criticism of Ben Jonson, whose style showed that he was careless of his future glory:

> Ben, old and poor, as little seem'd to heed
> The Life to come, in ev'ry Poet's Creed. (73–4)

Doubt is thrown on the old slogan *Vox Populi Vox Dei*:[40]

> the People's Voice is odd.
> It is, and it is not, the voice of God. (89–90)

Some of Milton's least inspired lines have to do with religion:

> In Quibbles, Angel and Archangel join,
> And God the Father turns a School-divine. (101–2)

A good-natured but unmistakable irony plays over the rendition of Sternhold and Hopkins' psalms by the choir of a children's charity school (230ff.), and there is a humorous reference to Whittingham's hymn, which began:

> Preserve us Lord, by Thy dear Word,
> From Turk and Pope defend us, Lord.

(That is Pope, of course, playing on his own name.)

In one respect Pope's technique is more limited in this poem than in *Epist*. 2.2. In the latter, as a means of elaboration, he uses not only Horace's *Odes* and *Ars Poetica* but also Lucretius, Juvenal, and the notes of the Delphin commentary on the epistle.[41] Here he seems to draw on very little outside the *Epistle to Augustus* itself.[42] However, he makes up for this by substituting mock-panegyric for real panegyric (as we have seen), and also by converting Horace's purely stylistic criticisms of earlier poets into a comprehensive satire (literary, political and moral) of the English court. Near the beginning of *his* epistle Horace complains that the Twelve Tables (an ancient code of law) and the Pontiffs' books are regarded as inspired literature – a wildly humorous exaggeration (25–7). Pope, however, chooses texts which did enjoy esteem in his own day, and he disparages two of them on moral grounds:

> Chaucer's worst ribaldry is learn'd by rote,
> And beastly Skelton Heads of Houses quote. (37–8)[43]

This is more than a condemnation of the writers themselves; for Chaucer was well known in court circles, and Skelton was once tutor to Henry VIII. Later, where Horace criticizes Plautus for his poor characterization and loose plot construction, Pope complains not only of technical faults in Congreve, Farqu'har, and Vanbrugh, but also of the *moral* laxity of 'Astraea' (Afra Behn) who 'fairly' (i.e., without discrimination, as befits the goddess of Justice) 'puts all Characters to bed' (291). The dramatist herself, at one time, did 'intelligence work' for Charles II's government, and so was connected with the court. Again, when Horace draws a light-hearted caricature of the Greeks after the Persian wars with their frivolous love of novelty (93ff.), the erotic language (*arsit, amauit*, etc.) is purely figurative. Pope, however, when speaking of the period of the restoration, starts with a broad hint about the monarch himself:

All, by the King's example, liv'd and lov'd. (142)

The same kind of language continues in 145–50 ('Gallantries,' 'Romance,' 'yielding,' 'melting'), and the situation is then summed up in a devastating couplet:

No wonder then, when all was Love and Sport,
The willing Muses were debauch'd at Court. (151–2)[44]

Arguing that the poet is of service to the community, Horace says that poetry teaches children how to speak. Pope adopts the same idea: 'What will a Child learn sooner than a song?' (205). He then adds

What better teach a Foreigner the tongue?

– a palpable hit at the Hanoverian king and his very limited English. Not content with that, Pope continues to defend the poet as follows:

I scarce can think him such a worthless thing,
Unless he praise some monster of a King,
Or Virtue or Religion turn to sport,
To please a lewd, or un-believing Court. (209–12)

Needless to say, such an attack is a free creation of the Augustan satirist's hatred. Finally, in 129ff., after speaking of the poet as a moral educator of the young, Horace says *inopem solatur et aegrum,* 'he comforts the poor and sick.' Pope, specific as ever, illustrates the point by a reference to Swift; but he begins with Swift's *political* activities – the pamphlets in which he supported Irish trade and resisted the introduction of a debased currency. These achievements are summed up in the lapidary verse:

The Rights a Court attack'd, a Poet sav'd (224)

– a line which, we are told, put Pope in serious danger of prosecution. He then goes on to praise Swift's charitable works for the poor and sick:

> Behold the hand that wrought a Nation's cure,
> Stretch'd to relieve the Idiot and the Poor.[45]

With this courageous moral and political focus, Pope's epistle could just as well be called a 'transformation' of Horace.[46] But, though it moves away so far from the original, Horace would surely have been delighted with this marvellous tribute to his own masterpiece, and he would have shared the enthusiasm of Austin Dobson, who wrote:

> So I, that love the old Augustan Days
> Of formal Courtesies and formal Phrase;
> That like, along the finished Line, to feel
> The Ruffle's flutter and the Flash of Steel;
> That like my Couplet as compact as clear;
> That like my Satire sparkling tho' severe,
> Unmix'd with Bathos and unmarr'd by Trope,
> I fling my Cap for Polish – and for Pope![47]

CHAPTER FOUR

Tennyson and Lucretius
Two Attitudes
to Atomism

Here we are studying a poem without a specific Latin model, but inspired nevertheless by a Latin poet – not by Virgil, whom Tennyson so loved and revered, but by one to whom he was related in a much more intimate and disturbing way, viz. Titus Lucretius Carus. When we come to consider the Victorian poem in detail, we shall have to ask how authentic a picture it gives of Lucretius' mind, and how much is invented and imported by Tennyson himself as a way of externalizing his own inner conflicts. But first we must recall the system on which the *De Rerum Natura* is based.

In fifth-century Greece, Democritus and the shadowy Leucippus had propounded a theory of the physical universe based solely on atoms and void. According to this theory, which was taken up and modified by Epicurus (341–271 BC) atoms, i.e., indivisible entities, were the constituent material of all things. They varied in shape, size, weight, and motion, but were in each category infinitely numerous. Invisible themselves, they entered into countless combinations to form the objects of sense, thus producing secondary effects like hardness, colour, and smell. They continued in ceaseless motion, even inside solid objects, thanks to the existence of void, i.e., totally empty space. All bodies underwent continuous change, partly because of this inner movement, partly because they were constantly bombarded from without, and partly because they threw off filmy images of themselves – images which rendered them visible by coming in contact with the spectator's eye. While the universe was infinite and eternal, our own world was neither. It had once come into being in a random way, and it would eventually dissolve, liberating its atoms to form new combinations. In this vast process of birth, growth, decay, and death the gods had no part. They had not created the world, and took no interest in its petty history. Dwelling in interstellar space, they enjoyed a life of ease and serenity, unmoved by prayer and undisturbed by disaster. Such divinities were hard to explain because, being eternal, they could not dwindle or dissolve; at the same time, since they were visible to men in dreams and visions, they must necessarily give off atomic images like other creatures. So one infers that in some strange way a god's atomic output was always equalled by his intake. But why, you say, include such ineffectual beings in your system at all? Well, Epicurus thought they had to exist; otherwise men would not have been able to visualize them and worship them from time immemorial. They did also have a positive function, in that they provided exemplars of blessedness which the wise could contemplate with benefit. Since, however, they could not be angered by human sin or folly, they did not hand out punishment, and so they could not be blamed for human suffering. By establishing this point Epicurus believed he had freed people from one major fear – the fear of the gods. He had also, he thought, removed the other major fear, viz. the fear of death, by proving that the soul, like everything else, was material by nature. It functioned as long as its atoms combined with body-atoms, but when, at death, this combination was dissolved, the atoms which had made up the living person were scattered once more, and all consciousness ceased. It followed that there was no such place as hell, and that stories of eternal punishment were simply fables made up by anxious or tyrannical men. Hence (it was held) death had lost its sting. As for life, sensible people would do their best to avoid all kinds of stress, including those caused by greed, ambition, and sensual indulgence. Erotic obsession should be avoided; but if this proved impossible, desire should be appeased with the least possible emotional disturbance. It was best to live quietly with one's family and friends, enjoying the gentle pleasures, not least those of philosophical study and conversation. Such an existence was the closest man could come to the life of the gods.

In his account of the nature of things Lucretius differs in certain points from Epicurus. He seems, for example, more concerned with the injurious aspects of religion than with its finer possibilities. Granted, he does mention the importance of entering temples in an appropriate mental state so as to apprehend the images of the gods (6.73–8), but far more often he stresses the futility of ritual and the dismal fears associated with it. Also, far from distrusting poetry (as Epicurus did),[1] he thought it made philosophy more attractive, and hence more effective; philosophy, for its part, conferred on poetry the weight and dignity of all-important truths. To be sure, readers have detected a tension at certain points between the disciple of an austere philosophical creed and the poet sensitive to joy and sorrow. Thus after responding to the awesome beauty of a Mediterranean night sky, Lucretius insists that there is really nothing awesome about it, since it has not been contrived by the gods (5.1204–10). Or again, after quoting with apparent sympathy the words of a mourner,

> insatiabiliter defleuimus aeternumque
> nulla dies nobis maerorem e pectore demet (3.907–8)

> we wept for you inconsolably, and no length of days shall ever take the eternal grief from our hearts,

Lucretius adds that such grief is senseless because the dead feel no deprivation. Just occasionally, too, he treats the gods as divine personifications of certain activities or functions (Venus as procreation, Mars as warfare, Earth as mother, Sky as father), because he was unwilling to dispense with the power of those age-old poetic symbols.[2] Yet these contradictions do not imply any wavering of commitment; in fact, it is too much to call them contradictions; at the most they are minor discrepancies which make the writer more, rather than less, interesting.

If we wish to find fault with Lucretius, it is fair to criticize his far-fetched picture of the gods (self-renewing and indifferent), his unrealistic notion that a mourner's sense of loss is relieved by the thought of the deceased's extinction, and his ethical quietism (someone, after all, must govern, and Epicurean communities depended for their peace on political stability). It is less fair to complain about his unconvincing attempt to take account of free will (atoms, he says, have a tendency to swerve unpredictably), or about his failure to explain the procreative urge or the origin of life; for none of those questions has been answered yet. Whatever his shortcomings, then, Lucretius does present for our serious consideration an eternal universe, omitting as superfluous the idea of a creator god. (And indeed, to call in a creator is, as one of Hume's speakers pointed out, an example of *obscurum per obscurius*.)[3] The ultimate dissolution of the earth is a doctrine with parallels in Stoicism and, of course, in modern science. We manage to accept it, assuming that we ourselves will not be here to witness that event. As for the loss of our identity in death, that is rejected with horror in the Christian tradition. But other philosophies (e.g., Pythagoreanism and Buddhism) have reconciled themselves to it. The Greek myth of Tithonus (on whom Tennyson also wrote a magnificent poem) exemplifies the appalling prospect of eternal decrepitude; but even eternal youth may come to seem less attractive the more one tries to think of it.

But even those who reject Lucretius' philosophy are usually willing to acknowledge his towering stature as a poet, and to accept *De Rerum Natura* as at least a major document in man's intellectual history. Like Milton's, Lucretius' style builds its grand effects over whole paragraphs, and does not lend itself to brief illustrative quotations. So I shall simply refer to a few of the most famous passages, starting with the Prologue, or what Tennyson calls the Prooemion. There, in the description of a spring day in the countryside, as flowers open, birds court, and herds bound across the pastures, we sense a huge feeling of joy, like that expressed by Haydn in his *Creation*. Soon after comes the appalling story of Iphigeneia's ritual murder (1.84ff.). As he describes the Greek leaders, with their mixture of pathetic ignorance and criminal folly, Lucretius gives vent to an indignation more lofty than Juvenal's and no less powerful. Many will recognize the clinching *sententia: tantum religio potuit suadere malorum*, 'such was degree of evil which religion could bring about.' In Book 5 we have the compelling story of men's gradual advance in technology and in social organization (*pedetemptim progredientes*), a story which denies, however, that there can ever be general progress in happiness until the gospel of Epicurus is accepted (925ff.). Book 6 provides some terrific descriptions of thunderstorms, earthquakes, and other forms of natural violence. Unlike these examples, the passage on sex in Book 4 is not a great poetic achievement; but its cool, somewhat satirical treatment of desire impressed Yeats (via Dryden) in the twentieth century as much as it impressed Tennyson in the nineteenth.[4] It is worth noting that in this passage, which is somewhat bowdlerized in Munro's translation, simple lust is less problematic than passionate love, because the latter produces far more emotional disturbance. As a final example, here is a famous section from Book 3, which is so central to our topic that I shall quote it in Latin. After rehearsing a whole series of arguments to show that the soul is material and therefore mortal, Lucretius begins his summing up:

> nil igitur mors est ad nos neque pertinet hilum,
> quandoquidem natura animi mortalis habetur,
> et uelut anteacto nil tempore sensimus aegri,
> ad confligendum uenientibus undique Poenis,
> omnia cum belli trepido concussa tumultu
> horrida contremuere sub altis aetheris oris,
> in dubioque fuere utrorum ad regna cadendum
> omnibus humanis esset terraque marique,
> sic, ubi non erimus, cum corporis atque animai
> discidium fuerit quibus e sumus uniter apti,
> scilicet haud nobis quicquam, qui non erimus tum,
> accidere omnino poterit sensumque mouere,
> non si terra mari miscebitur et mare caelo. (830–42)[5]

Like other great passages on human mortality, that asserts, but at the same time, by its majestic eloquence, contradicts our total insignificance.

Turning now to mid-nineteenth-century England, we find ourselves in an era of dynamic change which brought widespread strain and contradiction. For various reasons the country had been spared the revolutions which racked Europe in 1848. All could see the advances being made in industrial life. Wages rose, hours of work were reduced, health improved, crime diminished; locomotives and steamers were just the most conspicuous symbols of an inventive and forward-looking technology. The general feeling of security and hope was summed up by the Great Exhibition of 1851 – an event opened by the Prince Consort with a speech in which he looked forward to the unity of mankind. Perhaps because of all these improvements, the evils of squalor and disease which still persisted seemed all the more evident.[6] And though there had been no revolution, the country was not without a discontent which occasionally erupted into violence. Yet in the main the balance was tilted towards optimism. So too, in the world of ideas, in spite of the gloomy prognostications of Malthus, the idea of progress, which had begun in seventeenth-century France, was taken up in England, and (if we adopt J.B. Bury's scheme [1920]) was about to enter its third phase with the publication of Darwin's *Origin of Species* (1859).

In science, atomism had been revived by Gassendi in the seventeenth century, though he rejected Epicurus' views on providence and free will. The further discoveries of Boyle, like those of Lavoisier and Proust, were taken over and consolidated by Dalton (1766–1844), who showed that all atoms of a given element were identical, that different elements had different atoms, that chemical reactions brought about not a destruction but a rearrangement of atoms, and that compounds contained a definite number of atoms belonging to each of their elements. These discoveries were in their turn extended and modified by Avogadro (1776–1856). So the hypotheses of Epicurus, which were reached solely by criticizing his predecessors and observing nature, were now confirmed by experiment, though there was still, of course, no apparatus for observing the atoms themselves. In spite of their possible implications, these advances had little effect on religious belief. If the Almighty had chosen to make the world out of atoms, so be it. Newton himself, who thought that even light was corpuscular, remained a firm believer.

Research in another area, however, would lead to serious doubts. Building on the pioneering studies of Hutton and Cuvier, Charles Lyell published the first volume of *The Principles of*

Geology in 1830. The work was expanded in the following years, so that the twelfth edition of 1875 was a massive two-part study with 650 pages in each volume. In 1844 an anonymous work appeared entitled *Vestiges of the Natural History of Creation*. It started with an outline of astronomy, and then went on to describe the formation of the earth. Excellent illustrations showed the types of organism, in ascending order, that were found in each layer of rock. The author (R. Chambers, who like Lyell was a distinguished Scottish academic) withheld his name because he knew the book would cause anger and distress. At the same time, outside the academic establishment, other work of the same kind was going on. In Devon in 1846 William Pengelly managed to raise funds for an initial exploration of Kent's Cavern. The results were disturbing; for human tools were found alongside the bones of extinct animals.[7] Across the Channel, the gentleman amateur Boucher de Perthes made similar discoveries in a gravel pit at Abbeville.[8] Irritatingly, because they were not university professors, these two men found it very hard to attract attention and support. Eventually, thanks to Lyell, a group was formed in 1864 to excavate Kent's Cavern. Meanwhile, in 1858, similar evidence had come to light in Brixham Cave. As work progressed more tools were found beside the bones of sabre-toothed tiger, hyena, bear, rhinoceros, and Irish elk.

Taken together, these discoveries produced a revolution second only to that of Copernicus and Galileo. In 1845, when J.W. Burgon described Petra in S. Jordan as 'a rose-red city half as old as time,' he was expressing the commonly held belief that the earth was no more than 6,000 years old – a figure based on Archbishop Ussher's studies of the Old Testament.[9] But as the new geological knowledge spread, it became clear that palaeolithic man was far older than Ussher had thought, and the earth vastly more ancient still (current estimates suggest it was formed 4,500 million years ago). Worse was to follow. In 1858 the two natural scientists Darwin and Wallace both read papers to the Linnaean Society, presenting the evidence for evolution, and next year saw the publication of *The Origin of Species*. In the Introduction, which was a model of courtesy and candour, Darwin listed all his predecessors from Lamarck to Huxley, and then went on to expound his own theory of natural selection. Lyell's *Antiquity of Man* followed in 1863, a work which ran into three editions in the same year.

Now half of the Victorian mind was disposed to accept evolution, because evolution could be presented as a kind of progress. But the other half rebelled, asking 'How can this be squared with the Bible?' At this point a third great tributary flowed into the mainstream of Victorian doubt. In 1835 D.F. Strauss published his *Leben Jesu*, a huge 800-page tome which came before the English public in 1848, doggedly and devotedly translated by George Eliot. Strauss systematically compared the four gospels, analysing the nativity story, the miracles, and the different versions of Christ's burial and resurrection. The result was to call in question the uncritical acceptance of the New Testament as a whole. The ground for this new approach had already been prepared by Charles Hennell's *Inquiry Concerning the Origin of Christianity* (1838). Hennell, too, discounted the supernatural element, so that the survival of the soul now became 'a matter of speculation, instead of certainty.'[10] As for the ethical implications, Hennell wrote 'Neither Deism, Pantheism, nor even Atheism, indicates modes of thought incompatible with uprightness and benevolence ... The real or affected horror, which it is still a prevailing custom to exhibit towards these names, would be better reserved for those of the selfish, the cruel, the bigot, and other tormentors of mankind.'[11] Those two works were followed in 1863 by Renan's *Life of Jesus*, a study which also removed the supernatural dimension but became widely known because of its sympathetic treatment of Jesus as a man. At the same time the Old Testament, too, was coming under scrutiny, notably in Bishop Colenso's rationalistic study of the Pentateuch and the Book of Joshua (1862). And rationalism itself was put into historical perspective in the great synthetic work of Lecky (1865). Finally, at least a brief mention must be made of the psychological theories of Bain (*The Senses and the Intellect*, 1855) and Spencer (*Principles of Psychology*, 1855). These writings could be interpreted, rightly or wrongly, as pointing towards determinism[12] – a trend which would continue with Freud and the behaviourists of the twentieth century.

Now all this, of course, is the merest sketch. I have confined myself to influential books which may be assumed, on the authority of the poet's grandson, to have been read by Tennyson. How thoroughly he read them is open to question; for most of them are hefty volumes calling for stamina and a strong digestion. But he will certainly have got the gist of them, and he was on friendly terms with several of the authors. So he was well aware of the strains imposed on the beliefs of thinking men and women. When Darwin visited Farringford in the Isle of Wight, Tennyson asked him if his theories did not make against Christianity. 'Certainly not,' replied Darwin.[13] Yet, even if we grant that Darwin was being a hundred per cent sincere, certain awkward questions could not be avoided by others; e.g., if a duck's webbed feet were really the result of the reinforcement of certain mutations without which the bird would not have survived, how could that be squared with the idea that God had given the duck webbed feet in order for it to swim? Again, was it to be assumed that God had grown tired of the countless species that had become extinct? As for man, if he evolved from anthropoids, how could he have been created in God's image? And at what point in his evolution did he acquire a soul accountable to God?

Various responses were adopted. One was to stand pat, and ignore or deride what the scientists and critics claimed. Another was to hold fast to the incarnation, the atonement, and the resurrection (which were, after all, beyond empirical challenge) and to concede most of the rest; another was to 'redefine' belief in ever more sophisticated language, starting from 'the significant myth' of the garden of Eden; another was to relinquish Christianity while adhering to Deism; another was to suspend judgment, opting for agnosticism (a term invented by Huxley in 1869); and another was to profess a thoroughgoing atheism. Eminent Victorians were to be found in every category, and many shades of opinion existed among Tennyson's friends. One thinks of such men as A.H. Clough, Edward Fitzgerald, Benjamin Jowett, F.D. Maurice, Henry Sidgwick, and Leslie Stephen. The most striking position, perhaps, was that adopted by Winwood Reade, who wrote: 'Supernatural Christianity is false. God-worship is idolatry. Prayer is useless. The soul is not immortal. There are no rewards and there are no punishments in a future state.' He then added: 'The supreme and mysterious Power by whom the universe has been created ... that Unknown God, has ordained that mankind should be elevated by misfortune, and that happiness should grow out of misery and pain.'[14] A strange combination of progressivism and despair.

Tennyson himself had always been aware of contrasts. While his father was a parson of the gentlemanly eighteenth-century type, interested in scholarship and distrusting 'enthusiasm,' his mother was a devout evangelical, and his aunt, Mary Bourne, a fierce Calvinist. Though confident that she herself was among the elect, Aunt Mary foretold a less happy future for the young poet. When I look at you, she said, I think of 'Depart from me, ye accursed, into everlasting fire.'[15] For many years, we are told, Tennyson suffered from bouts of depression. It is not clear whether these were due to religious anxieties, sexual guilt, or general feelings of unworthiness and futility; but certainly a deep malaise is audible in the sonnet beginning 'When that rank heat of evil's tropic day,' especially when the writer speaks of being 'all sin-sickened, loathing my disgrace.' The same note recurs in *Remorse* (1827) and in *Supposed Confessions* (1830). Over the next twenty-five years or so Tennyson seems to have driven the fear of hell from at least the forefront of his mind. Certainly in 1855 he gave public support to F.D. Maurice when the latter was forced to resign his Chair at King's College London for rejecting the notion of eternal torment.[16] Yet, as we shall see, that may not have been the end of the matter. But whatever worries Tennyson may have had about hell, he was altogether more interested in the positive aspect of survival: 'I am ready to fight for *mein liebes Ich*, and hold that it will last for aeons of aeons.'[17] With this strong sense of personal identity he yearned for immortality and searched eagerly for assurance. Like Yeats, he dabbled in spiritualism, and he belonged to the Metaphysical Society for ten years (1869–79).[18] But while in his happier moods he managed to believe in the immortality of the soul, and often asserted that without such a faith life could not be endured,[19] his position was always precarious, and he was too honest to pretend that he had obtained proof. His vacillations are most evident in *In Memoriam*, which he composed over a period of fifteen years, expressing different moods and making no effort to reconcile their contradictions. The concluding stanzas envisage a continuing development for the human race, and they end by speaking of

> That God which ever lives and loves,
>> One God, one law, one element,
>> And one far-off divine event,
> To which the whole creation moves.

But later Tennyson thought that such ideas were overly optimistic,[20] and indeed the introductory stanzas, which were written after the poem was complete, already revert to a more cautious and wistful position:

> Strong Son of God, immortal Love,
>> Whom we, that have not seen thy face,
>> By faith and faith alone embrace,
> Believing where we cannot prove.

In regard to more worldly matters, Tennyson might proclaim the triumphs of progress:

> Fifty years of ever-broadening Commerce!
> Fifty years of ever-brightening Science!
> Fifty years of ever-widening Empire![21]

and speculate daringly about the future (one thinks, e.g., of 'The Parliament of man, the Federation of the world' in *Locksley Hall*, 128). Yet the slums and filth of the big cities, and the dreadful conditions in which men and women, and even children, worked, were painful reminders of how much still remained to be done. Now it is evident that many of the evils associated with Victorian London – the drunkenness, the violence, the sexual squalor[22] – were exacerbated by poverty. Yet to judge from the experience of our own distracted century, it may be doubted whether the removal of poverty (if that ever happened) would lead to the eradication of sexual misery in its various forms. As a later Victorian, who knew about sexual misery, put it:

The troubles of our proud and angry dust
Are from eternity, and shall not fail.[23]

Granted, we have little information about Tennyson in this respect, partly because, out of 40,000 letters collected after his death, 30,000 were deliberately destroyed. But we are told that, in spite of his attraction to Rosa Baring, which lasted about eighteen months (1834–35/6), he had never kissed a woman until he married Emily Sellwood at the age of forty-one. She was thirty-seven. The new calm and stability which now entered the poet's life were doubtless due to the affection and encouragement she provided. It would be rash to infer anything from the report that they soon went to bed at different times and, during much of their life, had separate rooms. But Martin (on what evidence I do not know) states that between 1868 and 1872 Tennyson was 'preternaturally concerned with the dangers of sexual licence' (1980, 481). We hear of an occasion on which he walked out of a ballet in disgust, complaining about the depravity of the age. There is also some testimony that in later life he was given to telling bawdy stories.[24] Apart from such flimsy and fragmentary evidence, we have simply the observable tension (elaborated by Joseph Gerhard [1968]) between the puritan tradition, which preached the suppression of the senses and an edifying morality, and the romantic tradition of Shelley and Byron, which gloried in the senses and attached little importance to social respectability.

Progress and its problems, the topicality of atomism,[25] queries about the history of man and his ultimate destiny, disputes about the moral status of sexuality – all these Victorian preoccupations were memorably foreshadowed by Lucretius. Now there is good evidence of Tennyson's early study of Latin – the translations of Horace, the precocious rendering of Claudian's *De Raptu Proserpinae*, the delightful little poem on Catullus' Sirmio, the lifelong devotion to Virgil. In fact, Tennyson was the last major English writer to have thoroughly absorbed Latin poetry and made it a part of his intellectual and emotional experience. (One recalls Yeats's bitter feelings of disinheritance in that regard.)[26] At Cambridge, Tennyson knew H.A.J. Munro, the distinguished Latinist, who brought out the first edition of his Lucretius in 1864. And one must not overlook the striking account given by F.A. Palgrave of a visit to Farringford: 'Late over the midwinter fire, reading the terrible lines in which Lucretius preaches his creed of human annihilation ... and perhaps those on the uselessness of prayer ... and the sublime but oppressive fear inevitable to the thoughtful mind in the awful vision of the starlighted heavens – so carried away and overwhelmed were the readers by the poignant force of the great poet that, next morning, when dawn and daylight had brought their blessed natural healing to morbid thoughts, it was laughingly agreed by all that Lucretius had left us last night all but converts to his heart-crushing atheism.'[27] One suspects that in some cases at least the laughter was a little uneasy.

And now to the poem. Behind Tennyson's *Lucretius* (published in 1868) lies the story, reported in the works of St Jerome, that maddened by an aphrodisiac Lucretius wrote *De Rerum Natura* in the intervals between his bouts of insanity, and subsequently committed suicide.[28] If the substance of the story is true, it can be made plausible by a minor adjustment: e.g., as the poet became more prone to fits of melancholy, a woman (his wife?) inferred that his condition had a sexual cause and tried to cure him; instead, she precipitated his death. If the story is a fiction, it could have arisen from a simple error of transcription or memory, whereby Lucretius became confused with Lucullus, who according to Nepos was driven mad in a similar way,[29] or it could have been made up by someone who noticed that Book 6 was unfinished, and that the last section dwelt on a morbid subject (viz. plague); the poet's indifference to sex might have been deduced from the dispassionate and rather clinical account of sexual intercourse in Book 4. After that, it took little inventiveness for a chauvinistic tradition to blame his death on a woman. In any case, Tennyson takes over the story *in toto*. To explain how the drug caused *bouts* of madness, he has it administered on a number of occasions ('and this, at times, she mingled with his drink'). In addition he calls the poet's wife Lucilia – a colourful piece of pseudo-scholarship which he might have found quoted in Lachmann's commentary[30] or heard about from Munro.

The Introduction starts with a sad picture of domestic disharmony. After the 'first fine careless rapture' Lucretius, we are told, continues to love his wife; yet it is hard to see how she can be expected to know this. When he returns 'from pacings in the field' he barely acknowledges her welcoming kiss,[31] engrossed as he is in problems of philosophy or composition. This opening situation is presented in a long Latinate period. Then, as the wife takes action, the pace gradually quickens. She procures a philtre which is supposed 'to lead an errant passion home again.' The phrase carries a hint, which will later become important, of an animal which has broken out of its confines. Such a philtre, with its associations of witchcraft and magic, stands for everything which Lucretius and his teacher opposed. Then finally the periodic style gives way to rapid parataxis: 'And this she mingled ... and this destroyed ... confused ... made havoc ... checked; he loathed ... woke ... and cried.' The operation of the 'wicked broth' (not far from 'witch's brew') 'Confused the chemic labour of the blood' and 'tickled the brute brain within the man's.' The first phrase is like a malign version of 'the ... genial heat / Of Nature, when she strikes through the thick blood / Of cattle' (97–9). In the second expression, 'tickles,' with its half pleasurable and quasi-erotic connotations, is a remarkable choice. Also, whereas in *Mort d'Arthur* (250–3) the human brain is by implication separate from, and higher than, the animal ('For what are men better than sheep or goats / That nourish a blind life within the brain, / If, knowing God, they lift not hands of prayer / Both for themselves and those who call them friend?'), here the human part of the brain is outside the animal part, like a kind of Darwinian accretion. The whole effect is graphically materialistic (almost like Lucretius without the atoms). After a night of wild storm, then, Lucretius wakes. Calm has returned to nature but, poignantly, not to him. He has no inkling of what is happening. So in puzzlement and anguish he cries out. And here his dramatic monologue begins.

> Storm in the night! for thrice I heard the rain
> Rushing; and once the flash of a thunderbolt –
> Methought I never saw so fierce a fork –
> Struck out the streaming mountain-side, and showed
> A riotous confluence of watercourses

Blanching and billowing in a hollow of it,
Where all, but yester-eve, was dusty-dry.

The opening exclamation, the parenthesis breaking in on the syntax, the violent 'struck out' (i.e., 'revealed'), the flood of liquid consonants, and the tumbling sequence of unstressed syllables in 'Blanching and billowing in a hollow of it,' the contrast of 'dusty-dry' which stresses the *suddenness* of the cloudburst – all convey the feverish agitation of a mind that is becoming unhinged. Yet the picture is but a frightened version of what Lucretius had described in *De Rerum Natura*, e.g., '[Winds spread destruction] as does the soft liquid nature of water, when all at once it is borne along in an overflowing stream, and a great downfall of water from the high hills augments it with copious rains, flinging together fragments of forests and entire trees ...' (1.281–4, Munro). Moreover, in spite of the impression of a mind barely in control, the narrative proves to be carefully structured. Thus 'Storm in the night!' (26) is taken up by 'Storm' (33); and it then transpires that the three occasions when Lucretius woke and heard the storm were preceded by three dreams, which are now recounted in order.

The first dream is of nothing less than the disintegration of the world. This shattering event, however far off it might be, was an important article of Epicurus' creed:

> [maria ac terras caelumque]
> una dies dabit exitio, multosque per annos
> sustentata ruet moles et machina mundi (5.95–6; cf. 2.1145–9)

> [As for sea, earth and sky] a single day shall give them over to destruction; and the mass and fabric of the world, upheld for many years, shall tumble to ruin.

But Tennyson's description of the world's collapse was prompted by a more powerful passage of Lucretius, on a rather different topic. Several lines are missing, but the thrust of the argument, apparently, is that if Stoic theories were true there would be a constant tendency for the world to fly apart:

ne ... moenia mundi
diffugiant subito magnum per inane soluta,

...

terraque se pedibus raptim subducat et omnis
inter permixtas rerum caelique ruinas
corpora soluentes abeat per inane profundum (1.1102–8)

lest ... the walls of the world should suddenly *break up* and fly
abroad along the mighty void, ... and the earth in an instant withdraw from beneath our feet and amid the commingled *ruins* of
things in it and of heaven (*ruins unloosing* the first bodies) should
wholly pass away *along the unfathomable void* ...)

Here now is Tennyson:

> terrible! for it seemed
> A void was made in Nature; all her *bonds*
> *Cracked*; and I saw the flaring atom-streams
> And torrents of her myriad universe,
> *Ruining along the illimitable inane* ...

I have italicized the points of contact. 'Ruining' is a rare word
found in Milton (*Paradise Lost*, 868), and 'the inane' is a literal
transposition of *inane*, 'empty space.' Lucretius, now awake,
acknowledges that this dream has come from his own conscious
activity ('that was mine, my dream, I knew it'), just as a sleeping
hound dreams of the hunt – another image from Lucretius
(4.991–2).

The second dream, initially, is based on history. It comes from
an earlier period – the age of Sulla, with its appalling massacres.
The victims' blood falls on the grass; but instead of soldiers
springing up (as in the myth of Cadmus) girls appear, like the
prostitutes who took part in the orgies of 'the mulberry-faced
Dictator'; so political disorder engenders sexual disorder. The
prostitutes are called 'Hetairai,' the Greek form being suggested,
perhaps, by the Greek of Plutarch, whose *Life of Sulla* mentions
his 'diseased propensity to amorous indulgence, and an unres-

trained voluptuousness' (Loeb ed. 2). That same biography records a comedian's description of Sulla's debauched complexion as 'mulberry covered with meal' (2.1). The massacres are recounted later, especially in 30–1. The dream is meant, I take it, to revive memories of Lucretius' youth. He would have been about fifteen at the time of the battle of the Colline Gate (82 BC) which was the prelude to Sulla's savage dictatorship. The ensuing orgies would have been a matter of common gossip. Such experiences would doubtless have preceded Lucretius' conversion to Epicureanism. Now, as his philosophy of quietism begins to crumble, memories of violence and lust come crowding into his dreams. Nor is he allowed to be just a passive spectator; for the *hetairai* fall on him and half suffocate him. Are we being asked, then, to think of these 'hired animalisms' not just as an adjunct of Sulla's court, but as figures from Lucretius' adolescent imagination? Are they even supposed to represent a preoccupation which has stayed in his subconscious mind, overlaid by Epicurean *ataraxia* but never wholly expunged? If so, that would, of course, be part of Tennyson's fiction.

If the first dream is of Lucretius as a disciple of Epicurus, and the second is a wider dream of Lucretius as a citizen of the Roman republic at the point where it begins its protracted death-throes, the third is the widest dream of all; it shows Lucretius as the heir of Graeco-Roman culture. The scene, again, is one of destruction – Troy on its last night:

> Then, then, from utter gloom stood out the breasts,
> The breasts of Helen, and hoveringly a sword
> Now over and now under, now direct,
> Pointed itself to pierce, but sank down shamed
> At all that beauty; and as I stared, a fire,
> The fire that left a roofless Ilion,
> Shot out of them, and scorched me that I woke.

The excitement, born of fear and fascination, is vividly conveyed by the multiple repetitions. The phantasmagorical vision centres on a sword. Whose sword? It seems to move by itself. Yet surely it must belong to Menelaus, who in Euripides' *Andromache* is accused of casting away his sword at the sight of Helen's breasts.[32] Yet Menelaus is not mentioned, whereas Lucretius is. So is he just a bystander ('as I stared')? Or has he somehow merged into the figure of Helen's husband? At any rate he does not escape. In this weird nightmare, flames shoot from Helen's breasts, scorching him awake.

Reflecting on these frightening dreams, the poet now addresses Venus. Can she be taking revenge on him, as she punished so many in the old Greek stories, for neglecting to worship her? Has she forgotten the tribute he paid her in his Prologue? (But this is a sophistical excuse, for, as he presently admits, the Venus of the Prologue was a poetical symbol of nature's procreative power.)[33] Inadvertently, by a slip of the tongue, he claims that his verses will outlast Venus – inadvertently, for of course Venus is immortal. But which Venus does he have in mind? If she is Epicurus' Venus, anger is contrary to her nature: 'the supreme power of the gods cannot be so outraged that, in their wrath, they shall resolve to exact vengeance' (6.70–2). If she is *not* Venus, and is amenable to prayer, let her restrain her consort Mars from the blood-lust 'that makes a steaming slaughter-house of Rome.' Now in *De Rerum Natura* (*DRN*) 1.29–30 and 38–40 Venus was begged to do just that, and was indeed pictured as embracing Mars. But that, too, as Lucretius now admits, was just a personified image. He was not referring to the mythological Venus – the Venus who loved Anchises and Adonis and dazzled Paris (the 'beardless apple-arbiter'). Likewise the Venus invoked in the Prologue was not the goddess in whose literal existence the masses believed. But what sort of excuses are these? If the Venus of popular religion really exists and is now punishing the poet, all these protests about symbolism only serve to confirm his guilt.

The poet's vacillations continue. The world of nature as described in his Prologue *appears* to be 'the work of mighty Gods.' But Epicurus has shown that really the Gods dwell apart, ineffably serene, in a place which Homer came nearest to describing in his picture of Olympus in the *Odyssey* (6.42–5; cf. *DRN* 3.18–24). And yet, if everything is made of atoms in temporary conglomerations, how can the Gods remain eternally stable? That, certainly,

was the master's teaching, which Lucretius meant to transmit to
his friend Memmius (*DRN* 1.25–7):

> Meant? I meant?
> I have forgotten what I meant: my mind
> Stumbles, and all my faculties are lamed.

Now comes a glorious description of the sun – 'All-seeing
Hyperion,' who

> slowly lifts
> His golden feet on those empurpled stairs
> That climb into the windy halls of heaven.

But really, as Epicurus has demonstrated, the sun sees nothing.
His vengeance on Odysseus and his men (Homer again) is a mere
fable.[34] He is not a god. The gods that do exist are 'careless of
mankind.'[35] But if they care nothing for man, why should *he* care
for *them*? Instead of trying to contemplate their peacefulness
from a world of pain, why not seek permanent release? By death,
the poet reflects, he would avoid natural disasters, illness, age,
and (worst of all) the mental decay which is producing these
morbid sexual fantasies – fantasies which penetrate to the
breast.[36] To Lucretius these filmy images are revolting. Why,
then, does his mind admit them? He still has enough rationality
to state alternative possibilities in Epicurus' manner: does he,
deep down, find them attractive? Or do they force their way into
his consciousness like a lawless rabble? Can the poet not cast off
such fancies, as a mountain rids itself of a hollow cloud? The
DRN speaks of hollow clouds (6.127 and 272), and of clouds
piling up on one another (186). Clouds collect on mountains
(466–7), are *like* mountains (189–90), and are actually *called*
mountains (490).

Now the scene changes (though the poet's wish remains the
same). If only he could do what King Numa had done in that
delightful fable of Ovid's (*Fasti* 3.285ff.). After a violent storm
Numa averted the wrath of Jupiter with the help of two wood-
land deities, Picus and Faunus. First he trapped them with a bowl

of wine; then he forced them to cooperate by drawing Jupiter out of the sky with their magic. At his coming the treetops of the Aventine quivered (*tremuisse* in 329), just as they do in Tennyson, 186. But even as Lucretius imagines the scene, Picus and Faunus merge into Nymph and Faun, and then into Oread and satyr. Now Epicurus had shown that, for genetic reasons, double-natured creatures like centaurs (and hence satyrs) could never have existed: 'nor can there ever be creatures of a twofold nature (*duplici natura*) with double body (*corpore bino*)' (5.878–80, cf. 2.700–6). Yet because fragments of horse-images, floating around, could become attached to fragments of human images, it was possible to *visualize* such beings. And now, in spite of Epicurus' assurances, the vision takes on a frightening and disgusting reality, as the satyr pursues the Oread.[37] Shameful-ly, the scene also arouses excitement:

> Catch her, goat-foot: nay,
> Hide, hide them, million-myrtled wilderness,
> And cavern-shadowing laurels, hide! do I wish –
> What? – that the bush were leafless? or to whelm
> All of them in one massacre?

So again Lucretius is torn by violent but contrary impulses. Pre-viously he has followed Epicurus' path of temperate enjoyment,

> But now it seems some unseen monster lays
> His vast and filthy hands upon my will,
> Wrenching it backward into his; and spoils
> My bliss in being.

Poetry has been his main reason for living – honey-sweet poetry through which he has conveyed bitter but wholesome truth. But now that his creative powers are failing, his thoughts turn to suicide. It will be a noble act, displaying his refusal to be 'dragged in triumph.' That idea makes him think (anachronistically) of Cleopatra.[38] And she in turn leads to the thought of another heroine's suicide – that of Lucretia. This thought brings a mo-mentary lightening of spirit, for by her death Lucretia (the poet's namesake) brought forth the republic, which has lasted for over four hundred years, though it is now shaking itself apart.

Taking comfort from the thought that his great poem will survive until the world itself disintegrates,[39] Lucretius nerves himself for his act of self-annihilation. Such an act was not forbidden in the atomistic tradition. Democritus took his own life (3.1039–41) – significantly when his *mental* powers had gone. Cicero's friend Atticus, when racked by an incurable disease, simply stopped eating.[40] If Lucretius held on, in the end Tranquillity, that passionless bride,[41] would receive him. But he cannot wait for nature to take her course, and like another famous heroine he plunges a dagger into his body – 'Thus – thus.' It was Dido who cried *sic, sic iuuat ire sub umbras* (*Aeneid* 4.660), 'Thus – thus I would pass to the world of shadows.' The female image of Tranquillity as a bride is not casual or irrelevant; and it is quite clear that Lucretius' suicide is a symbolic rape: 'out of season, thus / I woo thee roughly.' In that chaotic mind blood, sex and death are all intermingled.

Lucilia now breaks into the room. Distraught, she cries that she has 'failed in duty to him.' But it is too late for such thoughts, debatable as they are. The dying Epicurean summons up his final breath, and, clear headed at the last, answers

> Care not thou!
> Thy duty? What is duty? Fare thee well!

This ending represents a late decision in the history of the text. Previously the reading had been 'What matters? What is duty? ...' 'What is duty?' was changed to 'All is over' because *DRN* made no mention of duty. But then Tennyson reinstated 'duty,' and indeed reinforced it in the final version. Precisely because *DRN* says nothing about duty, Lucretius can be made to wave it aside. As for 'Care not thou!,' that too is the authentic Epicurean voice, offering no comfort to the mourner, and bleakly facing up to extinction. Lucilia, passionate, superstitious, remorseful about duty, is left to her grief. The poem ends, as it began, with a failure of comprehension.

Grove recognized Tennyson's *Lucretius* as 'one of the grandest of all his works' (Ricks 1987, Introduction). Should we not add that it is also one of the most extraordinary? To begin with, it is a superb technical achievement. I have mentioned that long opening period, which is syntactically quite complex; but the use of enjambement, and the varying of the pauses, prevent it from sounding stilted. The metre throughout, for all its regularity, includes a whole range of effects. Thus the interior monologue opens,

> Storm in the night! for thrice I heard the rain
> Rushing; and once the flash of a thunderbolt ...

In the first foot of each line a trochee has been substituted for an iambic, and the fourth foot of the second line is an anapaest ('of a thun-'). In 1.186 '(a riot) Strikes through the wood, sets all the tops –' not 'aquiver,' but 'quivering' – an unusual and effective tribrach in the final foot. In 257 '(man) Vanishing, atom and void, atom and void,' after an opening dactyl, two trochees alternate with two iambics, giving the equivalent of two choriambs 'atom and void, / atom and void.' The effect is that of wearisome and senseless infinitude.

Assonance and alliteration need no comment, but the dramatic variations in syntax are remarkable. Thus asyndeton sometimes imparts rapidity, as in the extremely compressed conclusion, sometimes emphasis, as in 'I hate, abhor, spit, sicken at him' (199). A combination of broken syntax, exclamations, and repetitions conveys terror or excitement or disgust (e.g., 26, 33, 46, 208–12). Repetitions, again, may supply a correction:

> lays that will outlast thy Deity?
> Deity? nay, thy worshippers. My tongue
> trips, or I speak profanely (72–4)

or steer the course of the thought:

> Which things appear the work of mighty Gods [i.e., Olympians]
> The Gods! [Which Gods?] ...
>   The Gods, who haunt
> The lucid interspace of world and world [i.e., Epicurus' Gods]

or deliberately blur the impression of rational control:

> [I] meant
> Surely to lead my Memmius in a train
> Of flowery clauses onward to the proof
> That Gods there are, and deathless. Meant? I meant?
> I have forgotten what I meant: my mind
> Stumbles, and all my faculties are lamed. (118–23)

Most of these examples dramatize Lucretius' increasing agitation. But there are also scenes of calm, as in the recollection of the Prologue of *DRN* (97–101), or in the picture of rural happiness (213–18, cf. *DRN* 2.29–31; 5.1392–4), or in the description of the abode of the gods (104–10, cf. *DRN* 3.18–24). And it is noticeable that, when the poet has made his decision, he gives a lucid and majestic exposition of his own annihilation and that of the human race (242–58). Here, for the last time, his mind regains its full power, and we have a masterly periodic sentence, including one of those long parentheses that are so characteristic of the *DRN*.[42]

Yet the technique, with all its facets, remains subordinate to the poem's overall purpose – namely, to portray the undermining of a great intelligence, an intelligence to which Tennyson felt in many ways akin. He admired 'the rise and long roll' of Lucretius' hexameter, his learning, his eager evangelical spirit, and the imaginative powers he displayed in his descriptions, not only of nature and men but also of the atomic world beneath the senses.[43] Like Lucretius, Tennyson rejected the crudities of Greek anthropomorphism, the divinity of heavenly bodies, and the more mechanical aspects of religious ritual. So much was straightforward. But in other areas his relation to his predecessor was more complex. First, although Lucretius recognized the precarious nature of political stability, and was keenly aware of the disorder of his own time (1.41–3), he did not admit to the *DRN* (whatever he may have felt) any doom-laden pronouncements about the imminent collapse of the republic. Such ideas are *imputed* to him in Tennyson's poem, as his rationality begins to falter (241–2). Political worries of a less extreme and apocalyptic kind may well have bothered Tennyson. We know, for instance, that there was widespread anxiety among the English upper classes about the possibility of anarchy following the Second Reform Bill, which was due to come into force in 1867.[44]

The situation is rather similar in regard to the treatment of sex. The puritanical side of Tennyson's mind will have approved of Lucretius' cool attitude to sexual relations, including the Latin poet's very Victorian pronouncement that wives should not move during intercourse (4.1268, 1277). But unlike Lucretius, Tennyson believed that desires which could not be satisfied within marriage should be suppressed. When, therefore, we read in Tennyson's poem about rampant *hetairai* and a satyr bent on rape, we suspect (rightly) that such fantasies are not drawn from the *DRN*.[45] We also suspect that the anguished poet's mixture of disgust and fascination suits the English Protestant far better than the Roman Epicurean, whose views on such matters were closer to the Cynics'. Once again such visions, which are 'strangers at [his] hearth / Not welcome,' can only be attributed to a Lucretius whose reason has been undermined by poison.

Now although Tennyson knew perfectly well he was using Lucretius for dramatic and poetic purposes, he may not have thought he was using him unfairly. He may have believed that Lucretius' morbid visions were not foreign to his mind, but rather latent; that they were not created, but merely released, by the witch's philtre. That possibility cannot be proved or disproved. What we *can* say is that Tennyson's Lucretius, in all his suffering, behaves with impressive dignity. When it occurs to him that he may be being punished by Venus, he does not grovel and beg forgiveness. He speaks up defiantly, and ends by reasserting Epicurus' conception of her. Later, aware that his mind is being destroyed, he blames this pugnaciously on an 'unseen monster' who 'lays / His vast and filthy hands upon [his] will.' And when he realizes that there is no way back, he refuses to acquiesce:

> Why should I, beastlike as I find myself,
> Not manlike end myself? (231–2)

He then asserts his humanity, and his Epicureanism, by suicide.[46]

There is one final question which may reasonably occur to us as we study the poem, though I have not seen it raised. Whether the visions have been plausibly or artificially imposed by Tennyson, why do we hear so very little about the fear of damnation? In the course of his long argument in Book 3, which is devoted to removing that fear, Lucretius allegorizes the punishments of Hades, and relocates them in this world. Thus the experiences of Tantalus, Tityos, Sisyphus, the Danaids (and Ixion),[47] and the punishments inflicted by Cerberus, the Furies, and Tartarus are undergone by the guilty in *life* (3.978–1023). In Tennyson, however, there is no such allegory. Lucretius' poem, it is said,

> stays the rolling Ixionian wheel,
> And numbs the Fury's ringlet-snake, and plucks
> The mortal soul from out immortal hell (260–2)

– an effect more often associated with the musical charms of Orpheus.[48] But why, as his reason becomes impaired, does Tennyson's Lucretius not have terrifying visions of the infernal torments which he has denied? One can only speculate; but a possible answer, in crude terms, would go something like this: we are dealing again with Tennyson's thoughts rather than those of the historical Lucretius. The Victorian poet had to decide for himself which was the more frightful prospect – total extinction, or survival with the *possibility* of hell. It seems that, although he had recurrent worries about hell, in the main he had managed to overcome them,[49] convincing himself, perhaps, like F.D. Maurice, that even for the most hopeless sinners there was no eternal fire but only separation from God.[50] As against this, extinction ruled out all possibility of eternal joy. Moreover, Tennyson occasionally expressed the view that to accept extinction entailed a lapse into brutalism:

> If Death were seen
> At first as Death, Love had not been,
> Or been in narrowest working shut,

Mere fellowship of sluggish moods,
　　Or in his coarsest Satyr-shape
　　Had bruised the herb and crushed the grape,
And basked and battened in the woods (*In Memoriam* XXXV, 18–24)

– lines which are highly relevant to *Lucretius*. If this suggestion
is right, then in making Lucretius contemplate his own destruction (and that of the world), Tennyson was bravely confronting
his own worst fear – a fear which in brighter moods he might
banish by an act of faith, but which he could never permanently
remove.

Lucretius is quite capable of standing on its own feet as an
imaginative dramatization of the Roman poet's last hour. Yet, as
we have seen, a lot of what Tennyson says is firmly based on *De
Rerum Natura*, and reflects a deep respect for the Latin masterpiece. Beyond these signs of direct affinity, however, a few important features are more Tennysonian than Lucretian; and, when
taken in conjunction with other testimony, they offer some striking insights into the Victorian poet's mind. One wonders, in fact,
if he knew how much he was giving away. Such revelations seem
evident to us now; but that may be largely due to one who was
only twelve when the poem was published – I refer, of course, to
Sigmund Freud. As for the Latin background, while the Augustan
Virgil offered a model of wholeness and poise to the poet laureate, it seems that an earlier, preclassical, writer could speak more
directly to the worried soul of a late romantic.

CHAPTER FIVE

Pound and Propertius
Two Former Moderns

In *Homage to Sextus Propertius* how did Pound re-present the Latin poet, specifically in the areas of imperial politics, love, and language? And how far were Pound's later statements consistent with this picture? Why has *Homage* evoked such conflicting responses? Is it partly because of disagreement about the nature of translation? Such are the questions addressed in this final chapter. A further, more general question has been consigned to an appendix, viz. whether the controversy about *Homage* has something to do with cultural changes which have taken place since the First World War, in particular the decline of Latin in the educational system, the development of certain critical techniques (applied in the first instance to English and American literature), and the general weakening of the sense of continuity in the Western tradition.

Imperialism and Its Poetry

The earliest surviving example of self-conscious modernism in Latin poetry is Catullus. Turning away from patriotic epic as initiated by Naevius and Ennius, he embraced the poetic creed, enunciated by Callimachus in third-century Alexandria, which had found its way to Rome by the 60s. According to this creed, the long Homeric epic, though magnificent in itself, belonged to a bygone heroic age. A sophisticated urban milieu called for shorter poems in various metres – poems which embodied a less austere, more private sensibility, and paid due attention to the complexities of romantic love. For Catullus, this was not just a literary stance. It was accompanied by a coolness towards Roman militarism; and it asserted the importance of fun, friendship and love against the traditional public virtues.

This attitude, which was taken over (though in a modified form) by Propertius in the 30s, is evident in three poems of Book 1. In no. 6 he addresses his friend Tullus, who is setting out for a spell of duty in Asia Minor. Propertius would like to go with him, but cannot withstand the protests of his beloved Cynthia. Tullus will help to impose his uncle's authority,[1] and to bring back justice to Rome's allies. Such concerns reflect his patriotic spirit. But may he never experience the pains of love! Propertius himself is unfit for military glory; he was born for active service of a different kind. So as Tullus travels on his mission he should spare a thought for his less fortunate friend, prostrate as he is, and committed to dissipation (nequitia).

Next (no. 7) we have an elegy addressed to the poet Ponticus, who is writing an epic on the age-old theme of the seven against Thebes – vying with Homer himself, as Propertius says with a smile. Propertius, by contrast, is composing elegy, which he hopes may be of use to himself and to other lovers. Elegy is a lowly genre; but Ponticus should be careful; for if he falls in love he will find that the mighty epic is of no avail. Shortly after, in no. 9, Propertius, somewhat gleefully, says, 'I told you so!' Ponticus has been smitten. Before things get any worse he should take up elegy; that gentle form will give ease to his wound.

Let us be clear about what Propertius is saying. In no. 6 he does not express any anti-imperial sentiments. Tullus' uncle represented Octavian's authority in Asia; Tullus himself has an important commission. But such work is not for the poet himself. In saying so he acknowledges somewhat ironically the official attitude to his lifestyle; it is a life of nequitia. In our elegant parlance, he is a worthless slob. Again, in writing to Ponticus, he does not run down epic per se. In fact, with a hint of irony, he emphasizes its grandeur so as to contrive a more dramatic reversal: once love has struck, epic descends, and humble elegy swings to the top.

We are dealing here, of course, with the tension between public and private values; and that may be said to underlie the whole of

Propertius' *oeuvre*. Over the centuries the upper-class view had been quite clear: whatever his personal desires, the individual was subordinate to his family; and his family, in turn, owed its position to the service which it had done the state. Religion was part of the same scheme; for the ceremonies of the state were often those of the home writ large. Marriage was an act of public responsibility, designed not only to perpetuate the family's name and property, but also to promote the welfare of the governing class and ultimately that of Rome itself. When, in the second century, the demi-monde emerged as a social group, conservative Rome accepted (with some reluctance) that young men would have recourse to them; but it was expected that such frivolous liaisons would be temporary – a prelude to the serious business of marriage and public service. The danger was that Amor, that wild and irresponsible creature, might inflict a kind of madness or disease upon the susceptible young man. What if he became enslaved to an accomplished *meretrix*, or worse still, to a Roman lady? Such enslavement would mean a loss of money and reputation, and would cause profound embarrassment to the victim's family. Catullus, we may be sure, was not the first such victim; but he was the first to demonstrate, in poetry which allowed no argument, that a passionate love affair could be a great deal more than a passing phase, more than a delightful but essentially frivolous adjunct to the serious business of life.

Propertius first comes before us as the heir of Catullus. When Book 1 appeared in 29 BC it attracted the attention of the great patron Maecenas – primarily, one assumes, because of its sheer poetic quality. There were no signs of enthusiasm for the new regime, but no expressions of opposition either. Like Horace, Propertius had suffered in the civil war. One of his relations had been killed in the siege of Perusia, and the family had lost much of its property. So he had bitter memories of those years. Nevertheless, Maecenas hoped that, like so many others, he would become reconciled to Augustus' rule, and that a writer of his talent might find room for themes other than *amor*. We do not know what pressure Maecenas, and later Augustus, applied. But even if little was said in the way of direct exhortation, Propertius himself could well have felt obliged, out of gratitude to his patron, to offer some formal acknowledgment of the regime and its achievements, even though the springs of his inspiration were non-Roman, non-public, non-political, and indeed non-moral.

Anyhow, whether challenge or problem, the new situation had to be faced. In Book 1 the life of an imperial official had been praised through someone else (Tullus), and the grander, more serious type of poetry had been acknowledged through someone else (Ponticus). But now Propertius himself had entered a kind of government service, and he was expected, on occasion at least, to retune his lyre. How could it be done? In formal terms he found a neat answer in his beloved Callimachus. The Alexandrian poet had refused to write a long poem on kings or heroes; in this he was obeying Apollo who had bidden him to keep his Muse slender and to avoid the highway trodden by the conventional and the pretentious.[2] This device, already used by Lucilius and others, could be developed in an adroitly diplomatic way. The poet could devote considerable space to patriotic heroes (especially the emperor), and enlarge on their praiseworthy qualities, before backing away and returning apologetically to his humble métier as an elegist.

Book 2 begins thus (in paraphrase): 'You ask why I write so much about love. I am prompted, not by Apollo and the Muses, but by my sweetheart. Her beauty and accomplishments inspire me to produce whole *Iliads*! Now if, Maecenas, I possessed a really *big* poetic talent, I would sing, not about traditional epic themes, Greek or Roman, but about the victories won by Caesar Augustus, with your assistance, in the civil wars from Philippi down to Actium and Alexandria. But, like Callimachus, I lack the lung-power to deal with such grand topics; it is my fate to sing of love.' The poet's preoccupation is described in a light, self-depreciating tone; the rejected stories from Greece and Rome are labelled in cleverly compressed phrases (19–24); and even the officially glorious events of the civil wars (to which we will return) are passed over in a resolutely non-tragic style (25–36).

Let us look for a moment at the earlier passage (19–24) and see what Pound has made of it. Had I the ability, says Propertius,

non ego Titanas canerem, non Ossan Olympo
inpositam, ut caeli Pelion esset iter

I would not sing of the Titans, or of Ossa placed on Olympus
so that Pelion might form a path to heaven.

Pound (v.2) says:

> Neither would I warble of Titans, nor of Ossa
>   spiked onto Olympus,
> Nor of causeways over Pelion.[3]

Possibly Pound thought first of Ossa 'piled' on Olympus; then by
association (with or without the aid of Pelion) he reached *pilum*
(javelin); from there he arrived at the amusing 'spiked.'

> nec ueteres Thebas, nec Pergama nomen Homeri,
>   Xerxis et imperio bina coisse uada

> or of ancient Thebes, or of Troy (Homer's glory), or of two seas
> coming together at the command of Xerxes

(the last reference is to the canal dug across the promontory of
Athos). Pound:

> Nor of Thebes in its ancient respectability,
>   nor of Homer's reputation in Pergamus,
> Nor of Xerxes' two-barreled kingdom.

'Two-barreled' could come simply from *bina*; but to take account
of *uada* (seas) one might risk the suggestion that *uada* had slid
into *uasa* (containers or barrels). In any case we are left with the
notion, however bizarrely expressed, of 'fire-power,' and hence of
military strength. It is pretty clear that Pound did not know of
Xerxes' canal.

> regnaue prima Remi aut animos Carthaginis altae,
>   Cimbrorumque minas et benefacta Mari

> or of the early reign of Remus or the courage of lofty Carthage
> and the menace of the Cimbri and the services of Marius.

Pound:

> or of Remus and
> his royal family,
> Nor of dignified Carthaginian characters,
> Nor of Welsh mines and the profit Marus had out of them.

The Cimbri, who threatened Italy and were defeated by Marius in 101 BC, sounded quite close enough to Cymru, 'Wales' (pronounced 'Cumry'), to give the 'mines' (*minas*) a Welsh locality. Marus, a representative of Roman economic imperialism, is, of course, a fiction. The whole passage turns Propertius' mild irony into a piece of clowning.

A similar 'send-up' of old Roman themes is found in Pound (II). In Propertius 3.3.7ff. the poet, according to Müller's text (printed in Sullivan), had dreamed of writing a patriotic work on such topics as the fight of the Curiatii against the Horatii, described in Book 2 of Ennius' *Annals* and in Livy 1.24ff.:

> et cecini Curios fratres et Horatia pila

and I sang of the Curian brothers and the javelins of the Horatii.

Pound:

> I had rehearsed the Curian brothers, and made remarks
> on the Horatian javelin.

Pound, one assumes, knew *pila* was neuter plural; but as he wrote he remembered another Latin word, *pila* (fem. sing.) = book-stall. He also thought of a later Horatius, viz. the poet Quintus Horatius Flaccus. So he added:

> (Near Q.H. Flaccus's book-stall).

The parenthesis may be a glance at Horace's patriotic poems, e.g., the Regulus ode (3.5). If so, Pound is once again embroidering on Propertius.

We must now step back a few years to a point before *Homage* was composed. On 14 August 1908 Ezra Pound hit town. He had £3 in his pocket and knew nobody; but with boundless energy and self-assurance he set about meeting everyone who mattered in London's literary world. He pontificated in a novel accent and idiom about poetry and art, advertising himself and dismissing others, but also (be it said) promoting a few whose work seemed to offer something fresh and original. Whether charming or irritating, he could not be ignored. Two features of his life in the next decade may be singled out as relevant here. First, as we follow his activities in the very detailed biographies of Stock (1970) and Carpenter (1988), we are struck by the almost exclusively *literary* nature of his preoccupations. There is virtually no comment on how people lived (their work, their homes, their sports and pastimes), nothing about religion or politics; and, most surprising of all, almost nothing about the appalling cataclysm of the First World War. *After* the war Pound inveighed against its mindless waste. But during the conflict he did his best to isolate himself (Carpenter 1988, 255).

The second point is that, having no roots, Pound was something of a nomad (Carpenter 1988, 23, 154). Initially at least, he seems to have lacked a clear sense of his own identity. Hence his wide-ranging but unsystematic reading in classical antiquity, ancient China, and medieval Europe may be seen in part as an attempt to acquire a poetic voice of his own. Now among the poets of the past the Romans held a special place. '[They] are the only ones we know of,' said Pound, 'who had approximately the same problems as we have. The metropolis, the imperial posts to all corners of the known world' (Paige 1951, 141). And among the Roman poets Propertius (as we have already indicated) seemed especially important for his treatment of politics, love, and language.

Although the operations at Actium and Alexandria were, strictly, only a prelude to what followed, Pound regarded them, with some justice, as forming part of Augustus' imperial record. And so we must look briefly at what Propertius says on those topics. Like many others, including Virgil and Horace, Propertius looked back on the civil wars with grief and horror (1.21 and 22;

2.15.41–6). Yet in view of what had happened since, it was clear that Augustus (whatever his early career had been like) represented Rome's only hope of recovery. In due course, with Maecenas' deft assistance, Propertius was won over.[4] This means that, while one may not sense any real enthusiasm for Augustus' victories (Perusia was an especially sensitive subject), it is a mistake to look for any criticism of the princeps. Thus in 2.1.25–6 Propertius writes to Maecenas

> bellaque resque tui memorarem Caesaris, et tu
> Caesare sub magno cura secunda fores

> I should tell of your Caesar's wars and achievements, and after
> mighty Caesar you would be my next concern.

He then goes on to speak of Mutina, Philippi, Naulochus, Perusia, Alexandria, and the triumphal procession in Rome, complete with the prows of Actian warships. Pound, who detects disaffection, says simply

> I should remember Caesar's affairs ...
>   for a background (v.2),

where the ellipses invite us to recognize a jarring *double entendre*. Later, in rendering the couplet

> nec mea conueniunt duro praecordia uersu
> Caesaris in Phrygios condere nomen auos (41–2)

> nor has my heart the strength to set Caesar's name in martial
> verse amongst his Phrygian [i.e., Trojan] ancestors,

Pound writes:

> And my ventricles do not palpitate to Caesarial *ore rotundos*,
> Nor to the tune of the Phrygian fathers.

One notes the ridiculous use of the medical Latinisms, the freshly coined 'Caesarial,' and the sarcastically applied phrase from Horace which is not in the original.[5]

It is part of Pound's thesis that since Propertius is anti-Augustan he must therefore be making fun of the patriotic poems of Virgil and Horace. Pound can be seen advocating this view of Virgil in section XII. There Propertius had said

> [iuuet]
> Actia Vergilium custodis littora Phoebi,
> > Caesaris et fortes dicere posse rates,
> qui nunc Aeneae Troiani suscitat arma
> > iactaque Lauinis moenia littoribus.
> cedite Romani scriptores, cedite Grai:
> > nescioquid maius nascitur Iliade (2.34.61–6)

May Virgil take pleasure in his ability to tell of the shores of Actium, over which Phoebus watches, and of Caesar's valiant fleet. He is now relating the stirring tale of Trojan Aeneas' arms and the walls he founded on the Lavinian coast. Make way, you Roman writers, make way, you Greek! Something greater than the *Iliad* is coming to birth!

Pound writes:

> Upon the Actian marshes Virgil is Phoebus' chief of police,
> > He can tabulate Caesar's great ships.
> He thrills to Ilian arms,
> > He shakes the Trojan weapons of Aeneas,
> And casts stores on Lavinian beaches.
> Make way, ye Roman authors,
> > > clear the street, O ye Greeks,
> For a much larger Iliad is in the course of construction
> > > > (and to Imperial order)
> Clear the streets, O ye Greeks!

Among other points, one observes the facetious transformation in the opening line, the assertion that the *Aeneid* is 'larger,' indeed 'much larger' than the *Iliad* (in fact, it is much smaller), the intentionally prejudiced gloss 'and to Imperial order,' and the sarcastic expansion of Propertius' good-humoured call to the Greeks to take second place.[6]

The focal point, however, for any discussion of Propertius' attitude to Augustan imperialism must be the plan to recover the standards captured by the Parthians from Crassus in 53 BC. In the event, the standards were retrieved in 20 BC without bloodshed, but in the preceding years there had been much talk of a military invasion, and it is this rumour which forms the background to certain elegies of Propertius. The tone and content of these poems oblige us to draw a distinction between the private love-poet and the public supporter of the regime. In the former capacity Propertius abhors war, with all its greed and cruelty; he plans for himself a life dedicated, first, to love, wine, and poetry, and later to the study of natural philosophy (3.5). And he ends the poem impatiently with 'You who find weapons more congenial – *you* bring home the standards of Crassus!' Again, he remonstrates with his relative Propertius Postumus, who is about to join the campaign. How could he leave his wife, Galla? Yet in spite of his heartlessness she will remain faithful and will welcome him home again like Penelope (3.12).

This does not necessarily mean that Propertius condemned the expedition on broader, political grounds. For all we know, he may have accepted the official view that enemies were best engaged as far away from Italy as possible, that the borders of the empire should be defended, and that the operation would be fully justified by its propaganda value, at home and abroad. But even if he believed none of these things, the client of Maecenas was certainly in no position to criticize or satirize the expedition as such. What he *could* do was to declare that others were better qualified to celebrate such projects (3.1.15–18); or to wish the Parthian expedition all success and a safe return (he would be part of the cheering crowd – along with his girl); or to claim that he *intends* to write a triumphal epic, but not yet (2.10); or (most ingenious of all) to promise something suitably grand if Maecenas, who has always eschewed grandeur, will give a lead (3.9). By adopting this rather playful, self-depreciating tone, Propertius sought to fulfil his Roman obligations without betraying his Alexandrian Muse. Other stratagems again are found in Book 4.[7]

Here, now, are two passages to show how Propertius handled
the theme; each is followed by Pound's version.

> surge, anima, ex humili iam carmine, sumite uires,
> > Pierides; magni nunc erit oris opus.
> iam negat Euphrates equitem post terga tueri
> > Parthorum et Crassos se tenuisse dolet.
> India quin, Auguste, tuo dat colla triumpho,
> > et domus intactae te tremit Arabiae.
> et siqua extremis tellus se subtrahit oris,
> > sentiet illa tuas postmodo capta manus (2.10.11–18)

Arise, my soul, from a lowly song; assume greater power, Muses;
there will now be need of a mightier tone. Euphrates now asserts
that the Parthian horseman no longer looks behind his back, and
regrets that he kept possession of the Crassi. Why, India offers her
neck to your triumph, Augustus, and the home of virgin Arabia
trembles before you; and if any land lies remote on the earth's rim,
that too will be conquered presently and feel the strength of your
hand.

Here is Pound (v.1):

> Up, up my soul, from your lowly cantilation,
> > put on a timely vigour.
> O august Pierides! Now for a large-mouthed product.
> Thus:
> 'The Euphrates denies its protection to the Parthian
> > and apologizes for Crassus,'
> And 'It is, I think, India which now gives necks to your
> > triumph,'
> And so forth, Augustus. 'Virgin Arabia shakes in her inmost
> > dwelling.'
> If any land shrink into a distant seacoast,
> > it is a mere postponement of your domination.

The abstruse and pompous ('cantilation'), mingled with the ba-
thetic ('apologizes for,' 'I think') and the overly literal ('large-

mouthed product') skews the passage away from its original tone, which is excited but not comic, and pushes it towards burlesque.[8] Finally, in 3.4.1ff. Propertius has

> Arma deus Caesar dites meditatur ad Indos,
> > et freta gemmiferi findere classe maris.
> magna, uiri, merces; parat ultima terra triumphos:
> > Tigris et Euphrates sub sua iura fluent;
> sera, sed Ausoniis ueniet prouincia uirgis:
> > adsuescent Latio Partha tropaea Ioui

Divine Caesar is planning to make war on wealthy India, and to cleave the waters of the pearl-bearing sea with his fleet. Great is the reward in prospect, men; the most distant place on earth has a triumph in store for you. The Tigris and Euphrates will flow beneath [Roman] sway. The province will come late under Ausonia's rods, but come it will. Trophies from Parthia will grow accustomed to Latin Jupiter's temple.

Pound's truncated version in VI runs:

> Caesar plots against India,
> Tigris and Euphrates shall, from now on, flow at his bidding.
> Tibet shall be full of Roman policemen,
> The Parthians shall get used to our statuary
> > and acquire a Roman religion.

Tibet, which is not present in the Latin, may owe its appearance to a confusion (conscious or otherwise) of *sera* (late) with *Seres* (the inhabitants of a region beyond India; the Chinese or neighbouring peoples). In line 4 the statuary travels in the opposite direction, and there may be a satirical, but historically misleading, hint of missionary work.

Up to now, in the interests of clarity, we have examined certain passages of Propertius on imperialism without reference to any of Pound's later statements. What, then, did Pound say? In 1931, fourteen years after writing *Homage*, he said that Propertius' elegies were written in response to 'the infinite and ineffable imbecility of the Roman Empire' (Paige 1951, 310). Later still, in 1938, he claimed that Propertius debunked the Augustan empire by 'slitting out its blah and its rhetoric' (Cookson 1973, 120). In writing thus of the regime, Propertius was 'twisting the tails of official versifiers, Horace and Virgil' (Carpenter 1988, 325).[9] To attribute such emphatically anti-imperialist views to Propertius is a wild exaggeration, unsupported by any evidence. We have argued that, on the least favourable interpretation, Propertius' praises of Augustus are lacking in conviction; but they certainly do not convey ridicule, mockery or satire. As for Virgil, I do not believe that Propertius' reference to the Aeneid (2.34.65–6) is anything more than good-natured, basically respectful, banter. As Professor Donald Davie, one of Pound's most learned and loyal supporters, observes, 'Pound coerces Propertius into avowing anti-Virgilian sentiments that in fact Propertius did not profess' (1991, 275). With Horace the issue is larger and more complex. Since the two poets do not name each other, it is tempting to conclude that they were not friends. That does not mean that their allusions to one another's work must point to personal antagonism, much less an ongoing feud. Such allusions can be interpreted quite satisfactorily as instances of *aemulatio*. That is the line taken by Flach (1967) in his very thorough study of the question.

What, then (to conclude this section), does Pound say about *Homage*? The poem, he says, 'presents certain emotions as vital to me in 1917, faced with the infinite and ineffable imbecility of the British Empire' (Paige 1951, 310). Combined with the fact that *Homage* was not published until 1919, that might suggest that the poem was unmistakably and damagingly an attack on Britain, an attack which held the British Empire responsible for the disaster of the First World War. Yet in fact only about a quarter of the poem has anything directly to do with imperialism. Moreover, the observations about empire are humorous. To be sure, tastes in humour are notoriously subjective; so there will always be disagreement about the success of those observations. Some readers, it seems, find them hilarious. Others, myself included, would place them more on the level of a juvenile spoof. But no one, surely, could regard *Homage* as incisive, hard-hitting, anti-imperialist satire. If the poem is judged mainly in political terms, as (thanks to Pound himself) it so often is, then it seems a strangely inadequate response to the disasters of 1914–17. Canto 16 and sections 4 and 5 of *Mauberley* are a very different matter.

Love

By talking so much about politics we have already distorted our picture of Propertius, whose chief interest was love, or the poetry of love. As a way of restoring perspective, it may be useful to think of him as moving in an area between Catullus and Ovid. When describing his feelings for Cynthia he can project an intensity which rivals that of the earlier poet; yet at the same time he often makes some rueful or sardonic comment on the absurdity of his condition. As we read through Book 1 we meet an obsessed young man who constantly finds new situations in which he can place his beloved – situations to which he reacts with a variety of moods. Thus we are shown Cynthia's dress and make-up, Cynthia about to travel overseas, Cynthia prevailed upon to stay, Cynthia on holiday at Baiae, Cynthia responding to the poet's imagined death, and so on. Propertius' wit is well illustrated in the third elegy, where he returns late after a party to find Cynthia asleep. As he gazes at her in his befuddled state, she assumes a heroic beauty rivalling that of Ariadne or Andromeda. Then suddenly she is wakened by a moonbeam, and at once the real Cynthia goes into action, shrilly berating her lover (without apparent cause) for his callous infidelity.[10] The affair continues through Book 2, then gradually becomes a less engrossing subject, and finally ends in recriminations at the end of Book 3. Nevertheless, the two retrospective poems about Propertius' love in 4 are the most interesting pieces in that book. In a sense the young poet was right when he said *Cynthia prima fuit, Cynthia finis erit* (1.12.20), 'Cynthia was the first; Cynthia will be the end.'

As a love poet, Propertius was by no means unknown in the 1890s. In his *Men of Assisi* (i.e., Propertius and St Francis) Lionel Johnson had written

Are the spring roses round thine head,

Propertius, as they were of old?
In the grey deserts of the dead,
Glows any wine in cups of gold?
Not all the truth dead Cynthia told![11]

Pound once admired Johnson. In his Preface to Johnson's poems (1915) he could still say that in a dozen places Johnson had left lyrics 'as beautiful as any in English' – high praise indeed. Then there was Ernest Dowson (1867–1900). His *Amor Profanus* is tinged with Propertius' melancholy – a mood which he found especially congenial; and he had used *Dum nos fata sinunt oculos satiemus amore* (Prop. 2.15.23) as a title.[12] While his best known piece had Horace's Cynara in its title, it was closer to Propertius in mood. There the poet yearns for a lost love in a period of futile dissipation during which he has 'gone with the wind.' When Pound took William Carlos Williams to meet Yeats in 1910, they found him reading 'Cynara' by candlelight to a small group of disciples (Goodwin 1966, 77). Much later, when Quiller-Couch was preparing the second edition of the *Oxford Book of English Verse* (1939), he chose the Cynara poem as the best example of Dowson's work. Pound knew Dowson's poetry well. In 1905 he had written a piece in his style (Carpenter 1988, 52); in 1908 he had addressed to his memory a poem called *In Tempore Senectutis* (King 1976, 50–1), and another entitled *Autumnus* (one of Dowson's pieces was called *Autumnal*). Pound's poem was written in the languid manner of the 1890s:

Lo the world waggeth wearily,
As gaunt grey shadows its people be,
Taking life's burthen drearily ... (King 1976, 249)

That second stanza sounds like parody (the first less so); but parody is by no means inconsistent with admiration.

Three years later Pound explicitly acknowledged Propertius in the Victorian Eclogue entitled *Satiemus* (King 1976, 157–8). In the centre we find these poignantly beautiful lines which reflect much of what then seemed most attractive in the Latin poet:

> The fair dead
> Must know such moments, thinking on the grass;
> Oh how white dogwoods murmured overhead
> In the bright glad days!

In the same year (1911), among his *Canzoni*, appeared *Prayer for his Lady's Life* (King 1976, 149), taken from Propertius 2.28.47ff. It begins

> Here let thy clemency, Persephone, hold firm,
> Do thou, Pluto, bring here no greater harshness.
> So many thousand beauties are gone down to Avernus
> Ye might let one remain above with us.

Now, as everyone knows, this was a way of feeling and writing which Pound was soon to reject. But such about-turns do not take place all at once. The collection called *Personae* (1909) already included a poem entitled *Revolt: Against the Crepuscular Spirit in Modern Poetry*. It began

> I would shake off the lethargy of this our time,
>   and give
> For shadows – shapes of power
> For dreams – men.

In 1911 Pound's free, but successful, version of the Anglo-Saxon *Seafarer* appeared; and in that same year he was calling for a poetry that would be 'austere, direct, free from emotional slither' (Eliot 1960, 12). Yet that was also the year of *Prayer for his Lady's Life*; and in 1912 there was still quite a lot of traditional diction in *Ripostes*. Nevertheless, new ideas were gaining the upper hand, partly as a result of much lively interaction with Ford Madox Hueffer, Wyndham Lewis, Yeats, and Eliot. In *Cathay* (1915), with its spare elliptical verse, the decadent languors of the 1890s were left behind; and *Homage* was written two years later. Pound was vividly aware of the change. Looking back on *Prayer for his Lady's Life*, he called it 'a perfectly literal and, by the same token, perfectly lying and "spiritually" mendacious translation' (Sullivan 1964,

9). In another letter (Paige 1951, 212) Pound fired one of many salvoes against the classicist W.G. Hale, who in the course of a critical review of *Homage* had translated *puella* as 'my lady.' 'What are we to say to the bilge of rendering *puella* by the mid-Victorian pre-Raphaelite slush of romanticistic "my lady"?' Fair enough, but had he forgotten the title of his own previous poem?

One other classicist came in for punishment. In his *Latin Literature* (1895) J.W. MacKail had written of Propertius in terms of 'the neurotic young man' (125), comparing his outlook to that of Rousseau in the *Confessions* and that of Goethe's Werther, and speaking of 'the abandonment to sensibility, the absorption in self-pity and the sentiment of passion' (126). This now infuriated Pound, perhaps because it stressed the very element in Propertius which he had once valued. Determined to enlist the Roman elegist as a modern, he did not just maintain that MacKail's view was 'partial' or 'incomplete'; instead he condemned him for failing to have '*any* inkling of the *way* in which Propertius is using Latin'; MacKail did not see that 'sometime after his first "book" S.P. ceased to be the dupe of magniloquence and began to touch words somewhat as Laforgue did' (Paige 1951, 246).

Now to single out Book 1 for its 'magniloquence' (even allowing for certain pentameter endings) seems very wide of the mark. But there was *something* about Book 1 – something which we sense at various points in those early pieces; e.g.,

> ei mihi, iam toto furor hic non deficit anno,
> cum tamen aduersos cogor habere deos (1.7–8)

> poor me, for a whole year now this frenzy has not abated; yet I am forced to conclude that the gods are against me,

or

> me sine, quem semper uoluit fortuna iacere,
> huic animam extremam reddere nequitiae (6.25–6)

> let me, whom Fortune always wished to lie prostrate, live and die devoted to rottenness.

Longer examples, e.g., 17.1–12 and 19–24, can be found; but the fullest illustration comes in that hauntingly beautiful, yet occasionally morbid, elegy, no. 19, which is too long to quote. The element I have in mind, of course, is romantic sentiment. It is not confined to Book 1, and even there it certainly does not exist on its own. Yet it does give that book a special colouring. This was acknowledged by MacKail when he said '[Propertius'] earlier work is at the same time his most fascinating and his most brilliant' (126). And Pound himself made a revealing remark, when in a letter to Orage (Sullivan 1964, 8–9) he said, with heavy sarcasm, that even Professor MacKail might have suspected that 'whatever heavy sentimentality there was in Propertius's juvenilia, it is not *quite* the sentiment of thirteenth century Florence decanted in the tone of the unadulterated Victorian period.' We infer, then, that Book 1 was ignored in *Homage* because at that stage Propertius was not quite ready for the twentieth century.

In the sections of Books 2 and 3 which *are* taken over, the sultry atmosphere of romanticism is dispelled, and a brisker air takes its place – one which brings out, in Eliot's words, 'an element of humour, of irony and mockery, in Propertius, which MacKail and other interpreters have missed' (1948, 19). Some qualification is in order here. MacKail who, according to Pound (Paige 1951, 245), was accepted as 'right' opinion on the Latin poets, had no particular authority on Propertius. The most perceptive and original work on that poet, and the most influential among students of Classics, had been done by J.P. Postgate (1881). In his introduction (lxxxvi–vii) Postgate says, 'occasionally he shews a vein of humour which we should not have expected; as in the description of the disconsolate lover's woes (1.16), of Cynthia's anger (4.8), of his own lack of courage (2.19) and of Hercules' perplexity in his thirst (4.9).' Although 'occasionally' is a vague word, this does imply that Postgate found some, but rather little humour in Propertius. When this is taken in conjunction with other testimony,[13] Pound turns out to be justified – at least to the extent (and this remains a major critical insight) that Victorian opinion of Propertius had got the balance wrong. Whether he himself got the balance right is another matter.

Let us examine a few presentations of the new composite Propertius / Pound. He will, I think, turn out to be an interesting but
uneven character. In Section III (Propertius 3.16) the poet has
received a summons to Tibur (Tivoli), where 'white hills display
their twin towers and the nymph of the Anio plunges into spread-
ing pools.' Pound opens well:

> Midnight, and a letter comes to me from our
>> mistress:
>>> Telling me to come to Tibur, *At* once!!

The glimpse of Tibur is cleverly made part of Cynthia's letter:

> 'Bright tips reach up from twin towers,
>> Anienan spring water falls into flat-spread pools,'

which is fair enough, for Cynthia was a *docta puella*. Then the
poet's anxious self-questioning:

> What *is* to be done about it?

Fine, but after that Propertius' nervous lover becomes unconvinc-
ingly prim and verbose:

> Shall I entrust myself to entangled shadows,
> Where bold hands may do violence to my person?

The picture of the lover's charmed life is well conveyed, e.g.

> The moon will carry his candle,
>> the stars will point out the stumbles,
> Cupid will carry lighted torches before him
>> and keep mad dogs off his ankles.

But then the balance is upset again, as the stilted pedant enquires

> Who so indecorous as to shed the pure gore of a suitor?!

This entirely misses Propertius' witty question:

> What villain would bother to stain himself with the paltry blood-supply of a lover?

One has the impression that Pound is no longer within the character, but is mocking it from outside.

In Section IV we meet the same kind of inconsistency.

> Tell me the truths which you hear of our constant
> young lady,
> Lygdamus.

So far so good. The English, though not idiomatic, and not an accurate translation, is intelligible on its own. But what is this?

> And may the bought yoke of a mistress lie with
> equitable weight on your shoulders.

The sense is so feeble that we have to turn to the Latin for assistance:

> sic tibi sint dominae, Lygdame, dempta iuga (3.6.2)

> then, Lygdamus, I hope your mistress's yoke will be lifted from you

(i.e., I hope she will set you free). So Pound has confused *dempta* (removed) with *empta* (bought), without any discernible gain. The next few lines are also clumsy; clarity is not recovered until

> Out with it, tell it to me, all of it from the beginning.

The description of the unhappy Cynthia which follows is entertaining and (given the ironic mode) not overdone. But then facetiousness takes over again:

> And a querulous noise responded to our solicitous reprobations.

It is not easy to see the point. People who overload their speech with Latinisms, though often pompous and boring, are usually correct. They would not use the plural of 'reprobation.' The next two lines are also awkward; in fact the second ('To say many things is equal to having a home') is nonsensical. But Cynthia's abuse of her witch-like rival is vividly expressed and enjoyable.

The lines in v.2 (= Propertius 2.1.1–16), which tell how Cynthia and her accomplishments inspire the poet, are very successful – as one might expect, since they are light-hearted in tone and not especially intimate. Section VI, however, provides a more interesting challenge. It begins with the incantatory

> When, when, and whenever death closes our
> eyelids,

from Propertius 2.13B. Then Pound cuts to 3.5.13–16:

> Moving naked over Acheron
> Upon the one raft, victor and conquered together,
> Marius and Jugurtha together,
> one tangle of shadows.

So in death (we conclude) two unimportant lovers will join the great captains.

> Caesar plots against India ... (3.4.1–6)

Such are the grandiose schemes of the great captains in life. But in death conqueror and conquered are on the same level:

> One raft on the veiled flood of Acheron,
> Marius and Jugurtha together.

This highly original effect, which is not incoherent, is produced by moving from 2.13B to 3.5; from there to 3.4, and then back to 3.5, after which the sequence resumes from 2.13B.

Now in 2.13B, as in 1.19, Propertius' mood is solemn throughout (that mood which so endeared him to the poets of the 1890s).

There is no hint of the modernist's wit. How does Pound cope with the piece? For a dozen lines or so he fares very well, describing the poet's funeral and Cynthia's part in it. The only snag comes in the verse

You will follow the bare scarified breast,

at which point one wonders why the dead man's breast should be bare and scarified. Turning to the Latin for an explanation, one finds that, of course, it is the mourning Cynthia's breast that is being described. A small enough point, perhaps. But then, as often, Pound seems to lose patience. The four lines on Propertius' cremation are omitted; then another dozen verses are cut – verses which portray the white-haired Cynthia visiting the poet's grave, and then proclaim the futility of long life, ending with the words of Nestor at the burial of his son: 'Death, why are you so late in coming to me?' Pound places the words 'Death, why tardily come?' just after the inscription on the lover's tomb. This, without any punctuation, causes bewilderment. There is a fine, plangent, conclusion:

In vain, you call back the shade,
In vain, Cynthia. Vain call to unanswering shadow,
Small talk comes from small bones.

That last line, with its wryly wistful play on words, stamps the version as Pound's. There is no such effect in the original.

A few comments now on Section VII, Pound's adaptation of that brilliant and powerful poem, Propertius 2.15. In a search for concentration, perhaps, Pound cut out some sixteen verses, which included a passionately felt condemnation of civil war. Yet his shorter version, apart from the first three lines, captures the excitement of the Latin very well – surprisingly well, perhaps, since (except for Endymion as 'bright bait for Diana')[14] it does not try to import any witty effects. At two points the weakness in sense, as so often, reflects a mistranslation. 'Let not the fruit of life cease' should be 'Do not leave the fruit of life to wither'; and the reader will wonder why stalks of flowers should be 'woven in baskets' (it is in fact petals which float in cups). But the main problem is confined to the opening lines:

> Me happy, night, night full of brightness;
> Oh couch made happy by my long delectations;
> How many words talked out with abundant candles.

Even after reading Davie's defence (1991, 78–9), it is hard to accept this translatorese. One assumes it is deliberate; yet 'the school-child's painful transliteration' has no place here; and the irony (whether derived from Laforgue or not) seems to be without point. Has Pound lost confidence in himself as a passionate lover? It is as if, in his embarrassment, he was assuring the reader that this was just a temporary role, and that really ole Ez don't hold with all that huggin' and kissin'. (He was, after all, raised as a Calvinist and a water-drinker.) But after that initial hesitation he forgets to be self-conscious, and all goes well[15] – a fact which may support what his biographer says about his late sexual development.

Carpenter (1988) draws attention to the lack of amatory verse in Pound's early work, interpreting this as 'a failure to engage in love.' This is confirmed by William Carlos Williams, who knew Pound well in those early days (56–7). It seems that although Pound kept company with a few women, and had, indeed, a propensity for getting into engagements and then drifting out of them, he was not especially keen on (or else was inhibited from) acquiring sexual experience. Even when he got married in 1914, there was some doubt as to whether sex played any part in the relationship (241). Three years later, however, an interest in sex does become apparent. Whether or not this was due to the un-usual conditions of wartime London, in which it was alleged to be easy to find a mistress, Pound himself said that he first had intercourse about 1917 (331), which was, of course, the time when he was writing *Homage*. Over the next few years he had a number of affairs. Nevertheless, unlike Propertius, Pound was not a man of a single dominating passion. And one of his fellow poets was not convinced that he possessed the real inner fire. Yeats found in him 'a single strained attitude instead of passion, the sexless American professor for all his violence' (504).[16]

Language

Those at home in this area will at once think of Pound's *logopoeia*, a phenomenon which he described as 'the dance of the intellect among words.' It employs words, he says, 'not only for their direct meaning, but it also takes count [*sic*] in a special way, of habits of usage, of the context we *expect* to find with the word, its usual concomitants, of its known acceptances, and of ironical play.' This is all very general, and (understandably enough) those who have tried to elaborate the concept theoretically have not always made it clearer. Also, in view of our own subject, one has to remember that the above passage was written over ten years after *Homage*.[17] So I suggest we forget about *logopoeia* for the moment, and without any reference to scholarly studies like those of Postgate (1881) or Tränkle (1960), simply jot down some striking locutions from those elegies which Pound used. Then, with the help of the *Oxford Latin Dictionary* (*OLD*), we can see what evidence there is, if any, for their novelty. Finally, we can turn to *Homage* to discover whether Pound perceived that novelty, and how he represented it. In preparing what follows I did, in fact, use that three-stage method. But for the sake of economy I present the first two stages together, quoting each phrase and at once giving the relevant information from *OLD*.

1 / Propertius 3.1.5 *quo ... carmen tenuastis in antro*? 'In what grotto did you spin your fine song?' This is the first occurrence of *carmen tenuare* (*OLD*, *tenuo* 1.b).

2 / 3.1.6 *quoue pede ingressi*? 'with what foot did you enter?' (e.g., curious, reverent, eager, hesitant?), *or* 'with what metrical foot did you enter?' (i.e., composing what form of verse?); see *OLD*, *pes* 5 and 11.

3 / 3.1.25 *quis equo pulsas abiegno nosceret arces*? 'who would know of the stronghold beaten down by the firwood horse?' Is the wooden horse pictured as kicking down the defences or as charging them like a battering ram? In either case there is humour in the oddity of the image (*OLD*, *pello* 1.a and b).

4 / 3.1.28 *Hectora per campos ter maculasse rotas*, 'that the wheels spattered Hector three times across the plain' (i.e., once for each circuit of Troy).

5 / 3.1.30 *Parin uix sua nosset humus*, 'his own land would hardly
know Paris'; the first instance of *humus* as 'an area or stretch of
ground,' (*OLD, humus* 3).

6 / 3.1.33–4 *Homerus / posteritate suum crescere sensit opus*, 'Homer
has noticed his work grow in later ages.' So Homer is somehow
aware of his own subsequent reputation. The phrase, of course, is
an ingenious reworking of Horace's *postera / crescam laude
recens (Odes* 3.30.7–8); *posteritate* on its own does the work of
postera laude, and according to *OLD, cresco* 7a, this is the first
example of a poem, rather than a person, growing in fame.

7 / 3.1.36–8 *illum post cineres auguror ipse diem. / ne mea con-
tempto lapis indicet ossa sepulcro / prouisumst*, 'I myself foretell
that after-my-ashes day. Care has been taken that the grave where
the tombstone marks my bones will not be neglected.' *OLD, cinis*
4b, gives this as the first case of *cinis* = death. Remarkable too is
the quasi-adjectival use of the phrase *post cineres*.

8 / 3.3.4 *neruis hiscere posse meis*, 'that I had the power to mouth
to my strings [the Alban kings and their deeds].' According to
OLD, hisco 2b, this is the first case of *hisco* with a direct object,
as distinct from an internal accusative. The indirect object is
also striking; *hisco* is being used like a grandiose equivalent of
cano.

9 / 3.3.9 *uictricesque moras Fabii*, 'the victorious delays of Fabius.'
Ennius' famous line *unus homo nobis cunctando restituit rem*,
or rather its sense, has been compressed into a three-word oxy-
moron.

10 / 3.3.13 *me Castalia speculans ex arbore Phoebus*, 'Phoebus,
watching me from the Castalian tree.' The other three instances
quoted in *OLD, arbor* 2, are clear collectives, e.g., *ager arbori
infecundus*. But the addition of *Castalia* makes the Propertian
passage rather different. One doubts if the Roman reader could
have avoided, at least initially, the idea of a god in a tree. Even
'the Castalian timber' is faintly comic.

11 / 3.3.41–2 *nil tibi sit rauco praeconia classica cornu / flare*, 'let it
not be your business to blow naval proclamations on a blaring
trumpet.' But as *classicus* can also mean 'connected with the
trumpet' (*OLD,* 3), its juxtaposition with *cornu* must surely have
produced the effect of a verbal play.

12 / 3.16.29 *aut humer ignotae cumulis uallatus harenae*, 'or may I be buried, walled in by heaps of anonymous sand,' the anonymity being transferred from corpse to sand.

13 / 3.6.26 *staminea rhombi ducitur ille rota*, 'he is drawn by the magic disc's threaded wheel'; the only recorded instance of *stamineus* being used thus (*OLD*, 1).

14 / 2.1.2 *unde meus ueniat mollis in ora liber*, '[you ask] how it is that my book of tender love is on everyone's lips.' Some scholars, however, in view of *mollis* (soft), take *ueniat in ora* in a more literal sense; hence, 'sounds so soft upon the tongue' (Butler 1905), 'sounds so soft upon the lips' (Goold 1990).

15 / 2.1.9 *siue lyrae carmen digitis percussit eburnis*, 'or if she strikes a song on the lyre with her ivory fingers.' 'Striking the lyre' is normal; 'striking a song' is a novel extension. Moreover, since Cynthia's fingers are as white as ivory, hovering near is the supplement 'like the plectrum itself.'

16 / 2.10.1 *tempus lustrare aliis Helicona choreis*, 'it is time to traverse Helicon with another kind of dance.' In plain prose, Propertius intends to write something martial and patriotic in hexameters. The idea of sacredness is present, but it is not easy to say how prominent it is. Does the phrase, in its literal sense, involve something like 'to lead a different ritual dance around Helicon'?

17 / 2.13.19 *nec mea tunc longa spatietur imagine pompa*, 'then let not my procession walk with a long mask (i.e., a long array of masks).'

18 / 2.13.20 *nec tuba sit fati uana querella mei*, 'let not the trumpet constitute a vain lament for my death,' an arresting predicate.

19 / 2.15.35 *quam possim nostros alio transferre dolores*, '[many strange things would have to happen] before I could transfer elsewhere my – pain.' One expects *amores*, though that is ruled out by the metre. *Dolores* is surprising, but characteristically Propertian; in fact, according to *OLD*, 2a, Propertius 1.10.13 is the first example of *dolores* = love-pangs.

20 / 2.28.4 *incipit et sicco feruere terra cane*, 'the ground begins to burn under the dry dog (i.e., the dog-star)'; a variation of the more normal 'the ground begins to become dry under the burning dog-star.' In Propertius' expression *siccus* strictly has the

unusual sense of 'parching'; cf. *sitiens Canicula* in Ovid, *Ars.* 2.231. The ordinary sense 'thirsty' is appropriate to a dog, but not to a star.

Such passages remind us that there is more common ground than is sometimes allowed between those who are supposed to regard every peculiarity of Propertius' language as 'interestingly poetic' and those who allegedly believe that every peculiarity should be removed by textual surgery. All the cases quoted above are in both Müller's text (1892) and Goold's (1990).

To conclude our experiment, let us see whether Pound noticed any of these innovations, and, if so, what he made of them.

(1) and (2): In Section I Pound has fastened on *choros* 'dances' (3.1.4). Taking *carmen* in its rhythmical aspect, he has acknowledged *tenuastis* by saying

Who hath taught you so subtle a measure;

assimilating Propertius' grotto to a dance-hall, he continues

in what hall have you heard it;

Then, glancing at both the primary and the secondary meaning of *pede*, he says

What foot beat out your time-bar?

For (3) he writes:

And who would have known the towers
    pulled down by a deal-wood horse?

That catches the tone well; the sound of *pulsas* has led to 'pulled' rather than 'battered.' Among several examples of this device are 'sitting' for *sitiens* (II), 'backwash' for *aqua* (II) (so Townend 1961, 43), and 'mines' for *minas* (v.2). Each case has to be assessed on its own. This one is very successful.[18]

At (4) Pound reverses the image: 'Hector spattering wheel-rims.'

So we have Hector spattering the wheels with blood, instead of them spattering him with mud. Though physically implausible, this increases the vividness of the horrible picture.

For (5) Pound writes:

> Their door-yards would scarcely know them, or Paris,

which ingeniously takes account of the unusual *humus*.

Pound has not paid any attention to (6). Perhaps he was misled by Müller's text, which fails to indicate that a new sequence of ideas begins at line 33. For (7), Pound writes:

> And I also among the later nephews of this city
> > shall have my dog's day
> With no stone upon my contemptible sepulchre.

Sepulchre without stone is a Christian interpolation symbolizing immortality. 'Dog's day' appears to mean something like 'hot-blooded life' (without the idea of temporariness which the phrase normally implies). In any case 'dog's day' has taken the place of 'after-ashes day' – assisted, one suspects, by the proximity of *cinis* to *canis*.

In (8), Pound exploits the basic meaning of *hisco* (I gape) to convey his dislike of grand verse: 'shall be yawned out on my lyre' (II). In (9), 'the victorious delay of Fabius' is striking enough to be left unaltered. So is the literal meaning of (10): 'looking upon me from the Castalian tree.'

At (11), Pound alters the sense to something quite different from (though not incompatible with) the Latin:

> Nor will the public criers ever have your name
> > in their classic horns.

Pound was quite entitled to slide from *praeconium*, 'declaration,' to *praeconius*, 'connected with a public crier,' if he wanted to. One just wonders what a crier is doing with a horn, classic or otherwise.

In (12), Pound (III) faithfully construes *ignotae* with *harenae*, apparently taking a swipe in the process at pettifogging bureaucrats:

> Or may I inter beneath the hummock
> of some as yet uncatalogued sand.

'Inter,' used intransitively, is also interesting. (It is not accepted American usage.)

At (13), instead of looking up *stamineus* (did he ever look up anything?) Pound seems to have used the visual image of a flower's stamen, and so to have reached 'spiked.'

In (14), Pound (v.2) has gone for something fairly close to the more vivid suggestions noted above: 'whence this soft book comes into my mouth.'

At (15), Pound (v.2) daringly renders:

> If she with ivory fingers drive a tune through the lyre.

At (16), Pound, in his reforming zeal, has gone far beyond the Latin:

> Now if ever it is time to cleanse Helicon (v.1);

but we did concede that *lustrare* contained some kind of religious nuance, and we are now familiar with the sight of Pound using Propertius for his own ends.

At (17), if Pound noticed that *longa* did not go with *pompa*, he must have decided that to link it simply with *imagine*, without any modifying phrase, would sound too eccentric. So he opted for normal usage:

> Nor at my funeral either will there be any long trail,
> bearing ancestral lares and images. (VI)

In (18), he abandoned the odd predicate, but made up for it by rearranging the Latin so as to form a paradox:

> No trumpets filled with my emptiness.

At (19), he presents Propertius' surprise without dilution:

Nor can I shift my pains to other (VII);

but why not 'another'?
In (20), Pound (VIII) writes

The dry earth pants against the canicular heat.

So the earth pants (dog-like?) under the heat of the dog-star.

However brief, the experiment indicates that in many of our twenty cases, Pound apprehended, and responded to, something novel in Propertius' use of language. It was surely this novelty, in its various manifestations, that Pound had in mind when he spoke of *logopoeia* – a term which might be translated as 'creativity in language.' (One suspects, however, that if Pound had been able to conquer his repugnance, he would have found a parallel novelty in Virgil.)

Yet, once again, the overall picture is not straightforward. Earlier, we observed how Pound led us to recognize Propertius' distaste for imperialism and its poetry, while at the same time claiming, quite wrongly, that Propertius' celebratory verse conveyed anti-Augustan satire. We have also noted how Pound rightly directed our attention to the wit and humour in Propertius' love poetry, but also how, in doing so, he sometimes lapsed into facetiousness and missed the romantic and occasionally sentimental side which had been overstressed in the 1890s. Here too, in his use of language (which many regard as the most interesting and original aspect of *Homage*) Pound presents a strangely two-sided picture. The problem centres not so much, perhaps, on Pound's competence in Latin (though one has recurrent doubts about that) as on his attitude to it. Let us move back to the beginning of the century. We are told that Pound left the Cheltenham Military Academy 'reasonably competent in Latin' (Carpenter 1988, 31). (According to Thomas's Appendix, he had three hours' instruction a week in the fall and spring semesters of 1901–2, six in the fall of 1902, nine in the spring of 1903; he then took three credits in 1905–6.) Stock assures us that Pound was able 'to read Latin easily and with pleasure for the rest of his life' (1970, 22). Even if we regard this as an exaggeration, the amount in *Homage* that Pound got *right* points to a considerable degree of control. Where he became lost, he could usually have obtained help from Gantillon's Bohn translation (1878) – a work which he might have treated with less condescension had he ever read it. But, as far as I know, there is no evidence that, Pound sought assistance from anywhere – translation, commentary, or even lexicon. Yet if he was as competent as that, why, then, are there so many hideous blunders in the *Early Poems* – blunders which begin with the dedication, and continue in quotations, epigraphs, and even titles?[19] The same carelessness is evident in the *Literary Essays* and the *Letters*.[20] Did Faber and Faber, one wonders, not employ an editor or proof-reader in the 1920s? Or can it be that Pound simply refused to accept correction? What are we to make of a man who claims to have a deep cultural interest in the Latin language and in certain Latin writers, who is eager to show off his expertise, and who yet seems to have no shame in his own use of Latin and doesn't have enough respect for his authors to quote them correctly? How different was the attitude of Yeats, who after causing satirical laughter in Dublin by the title *Speculum Angelorum et Hominorum* (an imaginary book on which he pretends to base *A Vision*, 1925) was acutely mortified and went into Trinity College to ask help from Louis Claude Purser, the editor of Cicero's *Letters*: 'For God's sake, Purser, find me an instance of *hominorum*!' Purser, who was a kind man, did his best, but failed.

Now if, in his earlier use of Latin, Pound had taken the trouble to be accurate, people would have been more willing to believe that the apparent blunders in *Homage* were really contrived to enhance the effect (as in many cases they were). But unfortunately Pound had not accumulated credit of this kind. Furthermore, over the years, even his friends noted aspects of his behaviour which in someone of less ability would have been branded as charlatanism. Carpenter points out that the jokey spelling in his letters 'had the advantage of cloaking his often genuine ignorance as to the correct form' (1988, 28); Eliot twitted him about his misquotations of Mallarmé (43); Aldington observed that 'Ezra was apt to get into ludicrous difficulties with his languages' (91). Aldington also made a revealing remark of a more general kind: 'He has tasted an enormous number of books, yet I doubt if he has ever read one with concentration from cover to cover' (43). This picture of superficiality bolstered by effrontery is supported by evidence about Pound's fencing: 'He was not well co-ordinated, and he fenced with wild unconventional strokes' (40). And William Carlos Williams describes the appalling effects of Pound the virtuoso pianist (61). One thinks of Algy at the beginning of *The Importance of Being Earnest*: 'I don't play accurately – anyone can play accurately – but I play with wonderful expression.'

Before *Homage* there were signs of trouble in other 'translations.' The Anglo-Saxon *Seafarer*, according to the expert Kenneth Sisam, was full of 'careless ignorance or misunderstanding' (156); there were similar complaints about Pound's versions of Cavalcanti (146) and his *Cathay* (267). But whereas few were qualified to compare those versions with the originals, many educated people in the 1920s had a grounding in Latin, and some in Greek. Such people were annoyed by the gap between Pound's linguistic pretensions and his performance. They also objected to the breath-taking arrogance of one who could dismiss Pindar as 'a prize windbag,' Thucydides as 'Fleet Street muck,' Juvenal as devoid of wit, and Virgil as 'a second-rater, a Tennysonianized version of Homer.'[21] All this helps to explain the very mixed reaction to *Homage* – a reaction which was to persist throughout the century.

There was also, perhaps, a formal reason for disagreement, in that no one quite knew how to classify *Homage*. It is not clear from Pound's letter to Iris Barry that he ever had in mind a conventional rendering: 'If you can't find *any* decent translations of Catullus and Propertius, I suppose I shall have to rig up something' (Paige 1951, 142). Anyhow, one cannot assume that what he had in mind then was what finally emerged. Yet in 1922 Pound seems to have claimed a high degree of fidelity – though the qualification which he adds does provide a loophole: 'I can so snugly fit into the words of Propertius almost thirty pages with nothing that isn't S.P., or with no distortion of his phrases that isn't justifiable by some other phrase of his elsewhere' (Paige,

248). Again, though in 1919 he insisted that 'there was never any question of translation' (Paige, 211, cf. 245), he frequently defended himself in terms which implied that he *had* been aiming at accuracy, at least of sense.

But if not a translation, then what? To avoid prejudice, Donald Davie would like us to ignore the link with Propertius and to read *Homage* as an independent poem (1991, 73). Most people, I think, would be happy to do that – at least for the first few readings. The trouble is that every now and then one comes on a line or phrase which can be explained only by referring to the Latin. Moreover, *after* the initial readings one is surely entitled to draw comparisons – as one is invited to do by the title. So the problem of defining the relationship remains. 'Better mendacities,' says Pound bitterly in *Hugh Selwyn Mauberley*, 'than the classics in paraphrase!' Used in its modern sense, 'paraphrase' is clearly too limited a term to describe *Homage*. Dryden offers more hope, defining 'paraphrase' as 'translation with latitude, where the author is kept in view by the translator, so as never to be lost, but his words are not so strictly followed as his sense; and that too is admitted to be amplified, but not altered' (Ker 1900, 1.237). Even that, however, does not allow the great freedom of method employed by Pound.

Closer still is Dryden's concept of imitation, 'where the translator (if now he has not lost that name) assumes the liberty, not only to vary from the words and sense, but to forsake them both as he sees occasion; and taking only some general hints from the original, to run division on the groundwork, as he pleases' (Ker, 1.237). This line is followed fruitfully by Sullivan, who mentions Pope's *Imitations of Horace* and Johnson's two great Imitations of Juvenal (1964, 21). Yet in one important respect Pound differs from Pope and Johnson. Apart from a few consciously humorous anachronisms, like 'erasers' and 'frigidaire patent,' he makes no attempt to assimilate Propertius to the contemporary world. We are still in the Rome of the 20s BC. Perhaps in the end we should settle for 'version.' Like 'imitation,' it has a respectable ancestry; and if we recall that *uertere* was applied to Plautus' adaptations of Greek comedy,[22] we may feel that the word has the right degree of elasticity.

The problem of classification, however, as we have seen, is just one factor contributing to the controversy about Pound. As the century comes to an end, that controversy may be losing its heat; nevertheless, to all except his enemies and his partisans, Pound, like his *Homage*, remains something of a puzzle. In presenting this puzzle, the foregoing comments may sound too much like the response of an indignant Latinist. So let me try to restore perspective. Even if we confine ourselves to the period up to 1920, there is much to admire in Pound's achievement. In spite of his more bizarre pronouncements, the man whose critical judgment was taken so seriously by Yeats and Eliot cannot simply be dismissed as a fraud. And the man who did so much to assist the careers of Frost and Joyce is more than the selfish egotist described by his detractors. Of his writings in this period, several of the shorter pieces can still be read with delight, and few would deny the originality and power of *Hugh Selwyn Mauberley*. His insight into the wit and verbal resourcefulness of Propertius have strongly influenced (though not, as some would have it, determined) our reading of that poet. More generally, Pound has brought an ancient writer to the notice of the twentieth-century literary public more effectively than anybody else could have done, and in a manner which no one else could have thought of. For all these reasons, and especially the last, he deserves our thanks.

Appendix

Professor Hale and *Homage* as a Document of Cultural Transition

In the earlier chapters of this book we have noted the freedom with which Chaucer, Shakespeare, Pope, and Tennyson treated their respective sources, and the extremely varied results. With Pound, however, something new takes place. It is not that he alters the spirit of his Latin 'model' (Shakespeare had done that with Plautus, and Pope with Horace), nor that he assimilates his 'model' to himself (Tennyson had created a composite *persona* of 'Lucretius-Tennyson'); it is rather that he plays around with words and phrases of the Latin original in a way which often causes bewilderment and at least *raises the question* of his linguistic competence. As we have argued, each case has to be taken on its own; and in the end the important question is not whether Pound misunderstood the Latin (though on several occasions he seems to have done so), but whether anything significant was gained by his departure from it. When *Homage* first appeared, even Eliot had misgivings about it: 'If the uninstructed reader is not a classical scholar, he will make nothing of it; if he be a classical scholar, he will wonder why this does not conform to his notions of what translation should be' (1948, 19). No wonder, then, that a classical scholar in Pound's own country should have found *Homage* disconcerting.

Students reading any account of the poem have probably come across the name of Professor W.G. Hale as an early critic of Pound's Latin. If they dip into Pound's *Letters* they will find him referred to as 'a god damn fool,' 'the ass Hale,' 'old brute,' and 'that fool in Chicago.' If, finally, they get as far as Hale's actual review (based on four sections of *Homage*) reprinted by Homberger (1972, 155–7), they will find a trenchant and witty article, written under the title 'Pegasus Impounded.' William Gardner Hale (1849–1928) was a Harvard graduate who, after studying in Germany, had returned to the United States. As a professor at Cornell and later at Chicago, he 'enjoyed a position of acknowledged pre-eminence among American Latinists' (Hendrickson 1928, 167) – a position confirmed by the honorary degrees he received from Princeton, St Andrews and Aberdeen.

Now I do not pretend to know anything of Hale's tastes in literature. He was probably rather better read in English poetry than the average educated layman.[1] (His review ends with a neat quotation from Browning.) But the area to which he directed his energies was not the appreciation of poetry, but something more fundamental (though not necessarily more valuable). Ever since the renaissance the primary business of a classical scholar, so it was held, was to produce the best possible text of his author. This called above all for expertise in language – a firm control of usage, grammar, syntax, and metre. Here Hale excelled. He published several articles on Latin syntax, and collaborated with C.D. Buck in producing what became the standard Latin grammar in America. Beyond that, he had the good fortune to achieve something which every textual scholar dreams of – in 1896 he discovered a manuscript. It was a manuscript of Catullus which had been wrongly described in a catalogue of the Vatican Library. This discovery led to a monograph: *The Manuscripts of Catullus* (1908).

Here, then, was a man who by 1919 had devoted half a century to studying the *ipsissima uerba* of Latin authors. Whatever the young Pound may have thought of such academics, the fact remains that, without Hale and a few dozen like him,[2] there would have been no Sextus Propertius for Pound to pay homage to. Hale therefore claims our respect. He also claims our indulgence; for he had never seen anything like Pound's *Homage* before. How could a literary man publish a version with so many careless mistakes? *Deliberate* departures from the Latin must have seemed even less comprehensible. In the four sections he read, he counted some sixty 'blunders.' How many of these were intentional is difficult to guess, for a rendering may be based on a misunderstanding and still provide some kind of sense. To illustrate the complexities involved I take one notorious example:

> carminis interea nostri redeamus in orbem,
>   gaudeat in solito tacta puella sono. (3.2.1–2)

After talking in the previous elegy about the divine power of poetry to confer immortality, Propertius here returns 'to the circuit of his song.' So his girl is expected to be 'touched' or 'moved' and to take pleasure in the familiar sound. As Messing points out (1975, 126), there is no evidence that the Romans would normally have contrasted a *tacta puella* with a *uirgo intacta*; here, moreover, *tacta* is obviously used as in 3.7.68, where Thetis is 'moved' by a mother's grief (*OLD, tango* 8). As for *in solito* or *insolito*,[3] Pound's version is ambiguous:

> And the devirginated young ladies will enjoy them
>   when they have got over the strangeness.

This implies that the young ladies will initially find the poems strange but will become accustomed to them.[4] Actually Pound is entitled to have it both ways; for he has altered Propertius' hexameter. He no longer refers to the poet's normal circuit; instead, ignoring the *re* of *redeamus* and construing *orbem* as 'world,' he writes:

> And in the meantime my songs will travel.

So he can emphasize the 'strangeness,' i.e., the novelty or originality of his work. It also makes sense, though a different sense, to interpret Propertius' *puella* generally (and ironically) as 'young ladies.' But why 'devirginated'? To judge from Pound's later remarks (Sullivan 1976, 8), the idea seems to have come from the combination of *tacta* (as opposed to *intacta*) and *delenisse* in the next line, where Orpheus is said to have 'tamed' wild beasts. Still, the implication of the jocose archaism is not clear. Does it mean that the girls will be (reluctantly) seduced by the poems and then subsequently find them agreeable?

In accounts of the Pound–Hale dispute Hale is often cast as the obtuse literalist against the perceptive poet who penetrates to the spirit of the original. There is some truth in this view, in that at the beginning of his critique Hale unwisely committed himself to the assertion that Propertius was never flippant. 'Never' is a risky word; it can always be refuted by a single counter-example. In Propertius' case the most obvious, though by no means the only, counter-example is 4.8, a parody of Ulysses' punishment of the suitors in the *Odyssey*, with the genders reversed. Nevertheless, Hale was not always wrong about Propertius' spirit. The four examples which he cites (155) show Pound not only altering the original but also lowering its stylistic register: 'I shall have my dog's day,' 'I shall have, doubtless, a boom after my funeral,' 'There will be a crowd of young women doing homage to my palaver,' 'There is no hurry about it.'

When we come to what an uncommitted reader might regard as Pound's sillier alterations, his advocates will tell us that his purpose was to make fun of Propertius, or to mirror the mental processes of the pupil who is struggling to learn Latin (Kenner 1951, 150–1),[5] or to ridicule the stilted diction of 'translatorese,' or to satirize 'the sort of person with a degree in Classics produced by British universities to run the Empire, a man sufficiently competent in Latin to get a bit of it right, sufficiently pretentious to produce a learned periphrasis, and sufficiently incompetent to subvert the whole point of a particular passage' (Davie, quoted with approval by Arkins [1988, 37]). Now Professors Kenner, Davie, and Arkins have read a great deal more Pound than I have, and they may be able to produce evidence for these statements of authorial intent. But the important thing for our present purpose is not whether such statements can be documented, but the fact that they can be made. The third suggestion is particularly revealing. That kind of resentment, which unfortunately is not without justification, helps to explain the, at times acrimonious, division of opinion about Pound and *Homage* which has existed since 1919. In discussing this matter it would be spurious on my part to pretend to act as an umpire; for in a very small way I have been engaged in the dispute. But I can try to describe the situation as fairly as possible.

In the period before the First World War the dominance of Classics in British public schools and grammar schools was already declining. New subjects were pressing for admission to the curriculum; and after enjoying a virtual monopoly for 400 years, during which the teaching was often disgracefully bad, Classics was slow to reform itself to meet the competition. In the postwar world of the 1920s and 1930s, people were less ready to accept the claims of tradition and authority, and in so far as Classics was associated (however unfairly) with the governing classes, the subject came under pressure. After 1945 these trends were accelerated. Then, in consequence of the Robbins report, a whole new range of students appeared in the universities – students who, however able, had little or no Latin, and certainly no Greek. It was natural, though unfortunate, that those who had been trained in Classics, and little else, should feel threatened (*après nous le déluge*), and should sometimes express superior disapproval of their Latinless contemporaries. It was equally natural, and equally unfortunate, that the latter should react with indignation. The most striking example of this resentment that I can remember was a distinguished Cambridge numismatist, who (c.1965) said he was so angered by the arrogance of classicists that he would not be sorry to see the whole subject collapse.

Now in the thirty years between, say, 1920 and 1950 the study of English literature (especially 'modern' as distinct from 'medieval') had developed far beyond its parent subject – not in the production of texts and commentaries (for in these areas classicists continued to produce distinguished work), but rather in the analysis and appreciation of poetry and fiction. These activities, which involved a reaction against romanticism, with its emphasis on the poet's personality, and a new concern with image, structure, and tone, owed much of their initial impetus to Pound and Eliot. And so an indifference to the modern critical techniques entailed an indifference to the two American poet-critics. Why classicists did not take the same path as their English colleagues is an interesting question. Partly, no doubt, they assumed (mistakenly) that as theirs was a deeply rooted subject, it did not require any radical reappraisal. Another related factor was that, within the classical syllabus at Oxford and Cambridge, literature, *vis-à-vis* history and philosophy, occupied a subordinate position. It also meant primarily the study of texts and scholarly problems; the place which might have been assigned to criticism was held by prose- and verse-composition – a gentlemanly accomplishment which had by now been elevated into a touchstone of scholarship. 'Critic,' in fact, was a title reserved for the emender of texts. Such men, especially on the Latin side (thanks to Housman?) often distrusted, and even despised, literary discussion on the grounds that it lacked rigour. It was as if, after restoring and cleaning a masterpiece, one should say, 'That's that; all the waffle about "meaning" and "quality" can be left to the journalists.' It was hardly surprising, then, that neither the dons nor their students had much to say about poetry as such.

The situation in America was less stark. Nevertheless if, for textual criticism and scholarly comment, one substituted the study of grammar, syntax and dialect, the pattern was not so very different. There too, conditions had not greatly changed since the nineteenth century. Pound wrote some telling pages on the matter in his 'Notes on Elizabethan Classicists' (Eliot 1960, 239–41). I quote two sentences: 'When the classics were a new beauty and ecstasy people cared a damn sight more about the meaning of the authors, and a damn sight less about their grammar and philology' (240). 'It is perhaps important that the classics should be humanly, rather than philologically, taught, even in class-rooms' (241). In the last thirty years that point has been taken. But sensible teachers know it is not a matter of *either* grammar *or* human interest. The trick is to get the proportions right.

This very general summary[6] cannot end without mentioning the name of F.R. Leavis. Born in 1895, Leavis served as a stretcher-bearer in the First World War, where, like thousands of others, he

> walked eye-deep in hell
> believing in old men's lies, then unbelieving
> came home, home to a lie,
> home to many deceits,
> home to old lies and new infamy ...

Back in Cambridge, and deeply scarred by his experiences,[7] Leavis cast himself in the role of the anti-establishment rebel. Speaking in a regional accent, and refusing to wear a tie, he did not conceal his dislike of older and more conventional teachers, with their upper-class manners, their Latin tags, and their deep respect for Milton. Leavis was not, by any definition, working class. His father sold pianos in Cambridge, and he himself had gone to the Perse School where, under the innovative W.H.D. Rouse, he must have acquired a fair knowledge of Latin. Nevertheless he accepted, and indeed cherished, the part of the injured outcast, attacking not only the personalities and opinions of his colleagues, but also their traditional scholarly equipment: 'The common result of a classical training (need it be said that there are, of course, exceptions) is to incapacitate from contact with literature for life' (134). The exceptions, presumably, included every critic from Sidney and Puttenham, through Dryden and Johnson, up to Coleridge and Matthew Arnold. The university responded to Leavis's behaviour by refusing to grant him appropriate status. He was not invited to join the Faculty Board until 1954, and he never held a chair. So with paranoid resentment on one side, and stiff-necked vindictiveness on the other, the hostilities remained unresolved. Many years ago (quite innocently) I asked that most humane of Latinists, Patrick Wilkinson, what Leavis was really like. (They had, after all, been colleagues for over thirty years.) 'Actually,' he said, 'we've never met.' Obviously the distance from King's to Downing was not measured in miles.

It was perhaps to be expected that the first sympathetic study of *Homage* by a Latinist, when it finally came, should come from America. This was a remarkably precocious article by L.J. Richardson, which appeared in 1947. In the early 1960s came essays by Edwards and Townend, followed in 1964 by Sullivan's excellent Introduction. A more critical, but not unfriendly article by Messing appeared in 1975. More recently there have been books by Thomas (1983) and Hooley (1988) and a generous endorsement of Pound's unorthodox approach by Arkins (1988). Such appreciations indicate that Latinists have now abandoned the totally negative view of W.G. Hale.[8] The sad thing is that, owing to the cultural transition mentioned above, the educated general reader is now rarely equipped to assess what Pound has done. Even in the recent past such assessments could be made by people who were not professional Latinists; and it has to be borne in mind that their verdicts were not uniformly favourable – see, for example, the pieces by Graves (1955) and Conquest (1963). If, with the help of Homberger, we survey the reactions of readers to Pound's work as a whole, including the *Cantos*, we will find a striking diversity of tone and judgment. This would suggest that, in the case of *Homage* too, a mixed verdict may be the fairest.

Notes

Chapter One

1 For evidence of Virgil's Epicurean phase see *RE* VIIIAI, 1043–4.
2 *Aen.* 2.294–5; 324–5; 619–20.
3 *Aen.* 5.700–3.
4 Aeneas' affections, though certainly less intense and less on view than Dido's, are nevertheless indicated in 4.266, 281 (*dulcis*), 292, 332 (*curam*), 336, 395, 440 (*placidas*), 448 (*curas*), 449 (though both Dido and Anna are also weeping, the terms of the simile suggest that the *lacrimae* are those of Aeneas); 6.455, 460.
5 See Horsfall 1990, 138ff.
6 Prescott 1963, 290, echoes Servius on *Aen.* 4.1.
7 *Aen.* 4.572–4.
8 For colonies at Carthage see Appian, *Lib.* 136; Plutarch, *C. Gracchus*, 10ff. (Caesar); Appian, *Pun.* 136; Dio 52.43.1; *Res Gestae* 28 (Octavian).
9 See Rudd 1976, 42–8.
10 On Dido see Otis 1964, 77 and 84. (There is a milder, but still critical, judgment in Quinn 1968, 325.) On Juno see Otis 1964, 79.
11 The anti-Punic *testimonia* are conveniently assembled by Horsfall (1990, 127f.). See also Burck 1943, 336–45. Horsfall speaks here and there of 'Roman feelings,' 'the Roman reader,' and uses the phrase 'to a Roman.' Now no one contests that there was vestigial anti-Punic feeling in Rome. But are we to believe that Roman opinion was unanimous and monolithic over four centuries? *A priori* that seems unlikely. Again, are we to suppose that a major writer like Virgil tailored his epic so as to reflect conservative opinion? Conversely, is it wise to assume that conservative, patriotic Romans

would necessarily have given the fullest and fairest interpretation of Virgil's text?

12 There are three 'pairs' of letters at the end of the collection: i.e., one of each pair is written by a man.

13 In her elegant and learned book Jill Mann writes of 'the glaring irony in Mercury's exhortation to Aeneas to hasten his departure because "woman is ever fickle and changeable" ... the phrase that became a proverbial expression of woman's fickleness has its origin at the heart of the classic story of male betrayal' (1991, 13). Naturally, no balanced reader upholds the generalization *uarium et mutabile semper / femina* any more than its counterpart 'men were deceivers ever.' In the context, Mercury uses the expression to precipitate Aeneas' departure for fear Dido will order her army to detain or kill him (see 566–8 and 592–4). The actual change he has in mind here is from grief, indignation, and wounded pride to violent aggression. It would be fair to talk of 'the classic story of male betrayal' if Aeneas had lost interest in Dido, or if he had simply exploited her from the beginning. But neither of these conditions was true.

14 Horace, *AP* 101–18, 125–7, 156–78, 310–18.

15 Sen. *Contr.* 2.2.12: *non ignorauit uitia sua sed amauit* ('he was not unaware of his faults, but he loved them'); 9.5.17: *nescit quod bene cessit relinquere* ('he doesn't know when to leave well enough alone'); Sen. *Nat. Quaest.* 1.278 accuses Ovid of descending *ad pueriles ineptias* ('to childish silliness'); Quint. *I.O.* 4.51 says he was *nimium amator ingenii sui* ('too fond of his own ability').

16 'He often writ too pointedly for his subject, and made his persons speak more eloquently than the violence of their passions would admit: so that he was frequently witty out of season,' Pref. to Ovid's *Epistles* (i.e., the *Heroides*).

17 Wilkinson 1955, 36, 39; Jacobson 1974, 8.

18 I have heard of it through Jacobson (1974, 8) and Riverside ed. 1059.

19 Printed in Austin's edition of *Aen.* 2, p. 295.

20 Anderson 1973, 55, 64. This idea is pushed further by Verducci, who contends that 'Ovid's heroines become "real" in so far as they become convincingly enigmatic' (1985, 32). But the problem centres on that 'convincingly.' It is hard to believe in a character who tosses off epigrams when writing a suicide note.

21 Hopkins 1988, 167–90.

22 For a good short account of how Chaucer came to the Latin poets see Harbert 1974. For his general relation to Ovid, see Fyler 1979.

23 On the French influence see Muscadine 1957 and Wimsatt 1974; on the Italian see Wallace 1985 and Boitani 1983.

24 For Chaucer's dreams see Spearing 1976 and Windeatt 1982. With Chaucer's agnostic stance cf. *Roman de la rose* 18469–84.

25 In *Aen.* 4.142ff. it is Neptune who calms the storm; Venus' plea comes later (227ff.).

26 Another trivial change. Chaucer has taken the storm from *Aen.* 5.8ff. There was no storm on the voyage from Sicily to Italy, thanks to the influence of Venus with Neptune (5.796ff.).

27 The gaps in the sequence are left by the omission of Ulysses, who returned to his wife, Hippolytus, whose behaviour was not dishonourable, and Orestes, who did not desert Hermione.

28 Cf. *The Book of the Duchess*, 731–4, where Dido appears briefly as an *exemplum*: 'Dido ... That slough hirself for Eneas / Was fals – which a fool she was' (for = because; which = what).

29 Shannon's book was reprinted in 1964. Since then, a number of writers have given (in my view) an inaccurate statement of the *Epistle*'s relation to the *Aeneid*. Delany, e.g., says: 'In the [Virgilian version] it is plainly the hero's obligation to leave his mistress, in the [Ovidian] he is blamed as a traitor' (1972, 48). A misleading antithesis. Equally misleading is the statement of Martin (1990, 194): 'The narrator points to Aeneas as a famous example of the "untrouthe" of men (*HF*, 384) ... But this interpretation is based on the version in Ovid's *Heroides*, not on Virgil's.' Helen Cooper says that Chaucer 'in several places ... plays off Ovid against Virgil to undermine the master-poet of Western cultural tradition, most strikingly in his retelling of the story of Dido' (1988, 72); again, 'Ovid gradually subverts the retelling' (73); 'the events of Carthage begin to be seen from the Ovidian perspective' (73).

30 The useful Penguin translation unfortunately gives 'mitigate' for 'excusen,' and 'a little' for 'fullyche.'

31 For the wider implications of this point see Minnis 1991, 2.41–51.

32 The comparison with the desert of Libya (488) was prompted by the African scene just concluded. For elaboration see Steadman 1961.

33 As Bennett points out (1968, 84), Carthage was the scene of Scipio's glory as well as of Dido's ruin.

34 E.g., its position between heaven and earth (715, 845–6), the sound like that of the sea (1034), and the rumbling of thunder (1039–41).

35 There is little evidence that Chaucer had read Horace (see Wrenn 1923). So it is worth asking whether Horace's *uitrea Fama*, 'glassy Fame' (*Sat.* 2.3.222) might have been known to him through some intermediate source, or whether the resemblance is just a coincidence. For *Fama* as a personified abstraction = renown, cf. *Odes* 2.2.7–8: *illum aget pinna metuente solui / Fama superstes; contra* Clemen (1980, 192).

36 See Evans 1930.

37 The classical author who is much the closest to Chaucer here, in both imagination and attitude, is Lucian, especially in his *Icaromenippus*, where Zeus is pictured sitting beside a succession of celestial man-holes, listening to the (largely discreditable) prayers ascending from the earth. It seems, however, that Lucian re-emerged too late to have been known by Chaucer.

38 This view, I take it, is quite traditional. It was already held in this century by Kittredge (1963, 106). Poetry, to be sure, is a recurrent theme in *HF*; but that hardly justifies attempts to turn the whole work into yet another *ars poetica* (see e.g., Shook 1968). It is good to see Boitani making this simple statement: 'There would have been no reason for Chaucer to call this a "Book of Fame" ... if he had not considered Fame its central subject' (1984, 14). The tightness or looseness of the work's structure is another matter.

39 In *Aen.* 1.633–6 Dido sends animals for sacrifice.

40 See the volume published by Musée Conde, Chantilly (text by E. Pognon) 30.

41 One approach to the problem would be that explored by Minnis 1986, 1.230–1, in connection with *The Franklin's Tale*, viz. to suppose that Chaucer is referring to Jupiter, who in certain authorities is regarded as the creator of the world. (The germ of the idea is already in *Aen.* 12.829, where he is called *hominum rerumque repertor*.) Yet it is hard to think away the Christian resonance of the phrase 'that God, that hevene and erthe made' (1039). Moreover, the conditional clause 'if that God ... Wolde han a love' etc. implies (I think) an exceptional circumstance, and therefore does not suit the licentious pagan deity. The alternative reading 'if Jupiter wanted a lady-love outside the usual range of his sexual interests' does not accord with the tone of the passage. On the Christian interpretation, if there is even a hint of a comparison with the Blessed Virgin Mary, that too is surprising.

42 It is true that *after* his final interview with Dido, Aeneas does leave by night (4.571ff.). Dramatically, what other possibility was there?

43 Talking of pity, I have often wondered how Sychaeus came to be present in the plains of mourning among those whom 'heartless love consumed with cruel wasting' (*Aen.* 6.442). Was it, perhaps, because Virgil could not bear to consign his heroine to everlasting grief, and so arranged for her to be comforted by her husband (473–4)?

44 See Riverside edition 1059, and Kiser 1983, 21 n.6. My own position is close to that of Ames 1986, 69–70, and Mann 1991, 32–4.

45 See Brewer 1978, 44, on 'Gothic femininity.'

46 To take an uncontroversial example, Horace treats Ulysses as a rogue in *Sat.* 2.5, but as an *exemplum* of admirable prudence in *Epist.* 1.2.18–26.

47 Professor Minnis reminds me of *The Legend of Thisbe*: 'Of trewe men I fynde but fewe mo / In alle my bokes, save this Piramus' (917–18).

Chapter Two

1 The first performance of *The Comedy of Errors* was on 28 December 1594. A free adaptation of the *Menaechmi* by William Warner (without the Prologue) appeared in 1595; it was reprinted, with the Latin text *en face*, by W.H.D. Rouse in the Shakespeare Library series, and by Bullough (1957, 12–39). Though Warner's manuscript had been handed round among his friends before 1595, there is no evidence that Shakespeare used it. Quiller-Couch and Dover Wilson (1962, 75f.) believed that Shakespeare worked from an intermediate play (*The Historie of Error*) which was performed on 1 January 1577. Most scholars, however, prefer the view of Baldwin (1944) that Shakespeare read the *Menaechmi* in Latin, possibly in Lambinus' edition (1576) and with the help of Cooper's dictionary (1565). While agreeing that Plautus was Shakespeare's main source, Salingar (1974, 66–7) is inclined to think that he worked *towards* Plautus from stories like those of St Clement and St Eustace, or that the farcical and romantic stories were present together in his mind from the beginning. Neither idea is incompatible with the present essay.

2 After greeting the audience, the speaker of the Prologue says *apporto uobis Plautum – lingua, non manu*, 'I bring you Plautus – on my tongue, not in my arms,' a mild pleasantry, extended in the appeal for attention which follows: *quaeso ut benignis accipiatis auribus*, 'kindly receive him with favourable ears.' He then assures

the audience that, unlike the writers of comedies who always claim that their plays are set in Athens, he will state quite frankly that the present piece takes place in Sicily – which it doesn't. Literal truth has been sacrificed for the sake of a verbal play, *sicilicissitat* being a Plautine concoction based on the Greek verbal ending -*ίζω*.

3 He steps into a *rapidum fluuium*, whereupon *rapidus raptori pueri subduxit pedes / apstraxitque hominem in maxumam malam crucem* (65–6). A lame translation would be: 'The swift-flowing river swept the legs from under the boy's kidnapper and carried him away to utter destruction' – lame, because *rapidus* bounces off *raptori*, *subducere* has the poetically just sense of 'steal,' and the phrase *in malam crucem* recalls the punishment meted out to criminals.

4 The nominative form Epidamnus occurs only here in the play. Shakespeare calls it Epidamnum.

5 Whatever innuendo may have been conveyed by the actor, the text contains no pun on *peniculus* = 'little penis.' Nor is the opportunity for such humour exploited later, when Menaechmus the Seeker asks Peniculus his name (498ff.). In 285 Messenio takes a *peniculus* out of his travelling bag. Some commentators assure us it is a clothes brush; others think it is a small sponge, the equivalent of a toilet roll.

6 Segal 1969, 147.

7 Perhaps 'half decent' is as far as we can go in view of 268, where Messenio is said to be a *magnus amator mulierum* (cf. 703).

8 See 1.1.132–6. 'Egeon,' a name found in Lily's Grammar, was doubtless chosen as being appropriate for a traveller in the eastern Mediterranean.

9 In Northrop Frye's fifth, or romantic, phase of comedy, 'the usual symbol for the lower or chaotic world is the sea' (1957, 184). Frye includes *The Comedy of Errors* and *The Tempest* as examples of 'sea' comedies. Very well; but it is in the romantic framework of the play that such symbolism occurs. There is no sea-rescue in the comedy proper, just as there is no sea-rescue in the *Menaechmi*. For that, or something like it, we have to go to the *Rudens*, which does contain a shipwreck, and hence prefigures *The Tempest*. One can talk of an *element* of romance in the *Rudens*, even though the romantic novel had not evolved as early as Plautus (late third, early second century BC). One can also talk, more generally, of *elements* of romance derived from Euripides, employed in Greek

New Comedy, and adapted by Roman playwrights. Such considerations, however, have little bearing on Shakespeare's specific debt, at that early date, to the *Menaechmi*. For the Greek original of the *Menaechmi* has been lost (see n. 28 below). Shakespeare had only Plautus' version; and the romantic element in that, as we have seen, goes little beyond the basic theme of 'lost and found'.

10 The Greek romances were ignored, partly because they were thought to be late (some as late as the sixth century AD), partly because the literary quality of the genre was not valued. Modern opinion tentatively dates the surviving specimens from the first century BC (the Ninus fragments) to the fourth century AD (Heliodorus). New translations of all the material are available in the admirable collection edited by Reardon 1989.

11 Heliodorus, ed. princ. 1534; French translation by J. Amyot 1547; Latin translation by S. Warschewiczki 1551; English translation by T. Underdowne based on the Latin 1569 (or 1570). Longus, French translation by J. Amyot 1559; English version of Amyot by A. Day 1587; ed. princ. 1598. Achilles Tatius, first complete translation into Italian by F.A. Coccio 1550; French translation by B. Comingeois 1568; English translation by W. Burton 1597. For a more complete list see Gesner 1970, 154ff.

12 The most recent text is G. Schmeling's edition (Leipzig 1988). Perry holds, with some others, that the original version was in Latin (1967, 304–5, 324). This view has not won general assent; but even if Perry is right, the novel is derived from the Greek genre in setting, structure, and ethos.

13 For bibliographical information see Gesner 1970, 155–7; an Old English version in an eleventh-century manuscript has been studied by Goolden (1958).

14 Quiller-Couch, xxiv.

15 One assumes that the goldsmith got his name from the gold coin called an 'angel,' which was first minted in the reign of Edward IV and bore an image of the archangel Michael.

16 Before he sees his patient the doctor inquires whether he is *laruatus*, 'possessed' (890). More indirect is the reference to pigs (289, cf. 314), which were sacrificed to secure release from madness.

17 For exorcism in the sixteenth century see Baldwin 1965, 37–46, and Greenblatt 1988, 94–128.

18 For the two varieties of hellebore (a drug used to purge the body of the supposedly harmful humour) see O'Brien-Moore 1924, 30–6.

19 'Thrice was I beaten with rods, once was I stoned, thrice I suffered

shipwreck, a night and a day I have been in the deep; in journey-
ings often, in perils of waters, in perils of robbers, in perils by
mine own countrymen ... in perils in the wilderness, in perils in
the sea' (2 Corinthians 11.25–6). How, one wonders, would the
saintly man have responded had he been told that his experiences
were the very stuff of fiction?

20 The germ of the idea occurs in *Men.* 600–1, where Menaechmus is
late for dinner with Erotium: 'She's angry with me now, I suppose;
the dress I gave her will calm her down'.

21 It was also, of course, from *Amphitruo* that Shakespeare took the
pair of look-alike servants. This increased the possibilities of misunderstanding. (False identifications in Shakespeare outnumber
those in Plautus by nearly three to one.) Moreover, with a second
set of twins and two parents all pretence at credibility is abandoned.

22 This cluster of ideas associated with time could have been suggested by *Menaechmi* 137–40, where Menaechmus hails Peniculus:

Men.   O mea Commoditas, O mea Opportunitas
          salue.
Pen.   salue.
Men.   quid agis?
Pen.   teneo dextera genium meum.
Men.   non potuisti magis per tempus mi aduenire quam aduenis.
Pen.   ita ego soleo: commoditatis omnis articulos scio.

('Hello! You're the very personification of all that's timely and
opportune!' 'Hello!' 'How and what are you doing?' 'Holding on to
my guardian angel.' 'You couldn't have come at a better moment
for me.' 'That's my way; I know all the nicks of time.')

23 A divinity like Isis or Artemis often presides over the characters'
fortunes. This divinity assumes a greater importance in Christian
romances like the pseudo-Clementine *Recognitiones*. See Perry
1967, Appendix 1.

24 A similar purpose is served by the mechanicals' performance of the
Pyramus and Thisbe story in *A Midsummer Night's Dream*; see
Rudd 1979, 185.

25 See Baldwin 1965, 1–17.

26 There do not seem to be any overt references to what Paul says
about the treatment of servants: 'servants, be obedient to them

that are your masters ... And ye masters, do the same things unto
them, putting away threatening' (Ephesians 6.5 and 9 in the Gene-
va Bible of 1560). However that may be, one notices that the two
Dromios collect far more in the way of threats and blows than
Messenio does – another example of Shakespeare being more Plautine than Plautus himself.

27 Cf. 110ff.

28 We do not know what play the *Menaechmi* is based on. At least
five comedies were entitled 'Male Twins' and one was called
'Doubles'. See Edmonds 1959 and 1961, 2.50, 396, 594, 626; 3.236
and 274.

Chapter Three

1 Horace, *Odes* 2.15 and 18.

2 See Mack 1969.

3 Cicero, *Fam*.11.20.1; 11.21.1. The real political dangers are made
clear by Appian 3.9.64.

4 Syme 1939, 192.

5 A dictum of George Long's, quoted with approval by Rice-Holmes
1928, 71.

6 Zanker 1990, 42; cf. Zanker and Vierneisel 1979, no. 82.

7 Analogous points can be made about the temple of Apollo; see
Taylor 1931, 153f.

8 For the cult of Augustus see Taylor 1931, 143ff.; for the east see
Price 1984, 54ff.; and for the west see Fishwick 1987, 80ff.

9 See Syme 1939, 486–9. For his earlier tolerance of attack see
Suetonius 55, 56, and 51.

10 According to the one British historian with a comparable reputation Syme's book shows 'a violent prejudice against Augustus'
(Jones 1977, 187). This seems to me to be less true of the later
sections of Syme's book. Certainly the final chapter is not unfair.

11 The figure includes two odes in which Augustus is not actually
mentioned (3.6 and 3.24), and five in which he is given four lines
or less.

12 Suetonius, *Life of Horace* (Loeb edition, vol. 2, p. 488). Augustus'
wisecrack proved over the centuries to be abundantly justified.

13 See those two deeply felt stanzas in *Odes* 2.1.29–36.

14 Dryden, ed. Ker (1900, 2.16).

15 The epigraph reads *ne Rubeam, pingui donatus munere*, 'may I not
flush on being presented with a crass and fulsome tribute' (*Epist.*

2.1.267). The editors do not explain its relevance. Perhaps we are to understand 'If I were king, I would not want to flush' etc., in which case Pope may be saying 'I'll make sure he does not get a crass and fulsome tribute from me.'

16 Taking a broad and impartial view Williams can claim that 'there was more personal and political liberty than under the alternative dynasty' (1974, 43). But the *Craftsman's* view was neither broad nor impartial; nor was that of James Thomson. See McKillop 1949 and note 23 below.

17 If being 'a Patron of poets in general' includes *listening* to their work, then Augustus satisfied that criterion. But that is to be distinguished from allowing himself *to be named* by all and sundry – a practice which he was keen to prevent (Suetonius, 89.3). This distinction is neglected by Pope. Shortly after, however, Pope draws a distinction which is not present in Horace. He separates the Town 'whose humour it was to magnify the authors of the preceding Age' from 'the Court and Nobility, who encouraged only the writers for the Theatre.' But the *populus* (18) which overvalues archaic poets includes prominent critics (50–1); conversely, the audience which packs the theatre for performances of the early dramatists (60–1) is not made up solely of 'the Court and the Nobility.' As for the vulgar pageants, the better classes (*equites*) are now just as keen on these as are the plebs (186–8). In saying this, Horace is not deterred by the fact that Augustus too enjoyed such entertainment (Suetonius, 45.2–3). None of this has any bearing on Weinbrot's theory.

There is a widespread belief that Augustus was especially partial to *early* Latin poetry, comedy in particular. This is stated without argument by Fraenkel (1957, 396 n.1), who refers to Madvig, and by Brink (1982, 563 n.1), who refers to Fraenkel. But there is no argument in Madvig either. As far as I can discover, the assertion rests on no authority. The passage of Suetonius which is cited in this connection is explicitly concerned with Augustus' command of *Greek* (89.1). So when the emperor is said to have enjoyed Old Comedy and to have laid on productions of it, that (however surprisingly) must mean Aristophanes, not Plautus. In his own literary style Augustus is said to have avoided both archaism and innovation (86).

18 Of two more recent writers on the same topic, Stack (1985), though frequently informative, tries (it seems to me) to keep too many balls in the air at once. One can hardly follow Dacier (who thought

Horace was praising Augustus) *and* Shaftesbury (who thought Horace was satirizing Augustus) *and* Weinbrot (who thought Pope was satirising both). To see Pope's satire as putting the reader into a pleasant state of bemused indecision is a late twentieth century view. Fuchs (1989), while acknowledging the corrective value of Weinbrot's book, declines to accept its thesis.

19 Like Horace, Pope avoids using the name 'Augustus' in his poem; but 'To Augustus' was added as a subtitle in 1751. Quotations are from the Twickenham edition; but the following errors should be noted in the Latin text; for *periise* (80) read *periisse*; for *Carmina* (138) read *Carmine*; for *pertorrita* (192) read *petorrita*; for *magnus* (213) read *magus*; for *tamen* (238) read *tam*. None of these slips is present in Heinsius' edition (Leiden 1629), which according to Bloom (1964) was Pope's basic text, or in the edition of Desprez. In the English text, for Poet's (294) read Poets; 'The apostrophe in the plural (s') did not become regular till about the end of the century,' *The Poems of Samuel Johnson*, 2d ed., Oxford 1974, 35 n.36.

20 So Weinbrot 1978, 244; see his references.

21 In particular Pope is referring to the searches conducted by the Spanish in West Indian waters. See Williams 1974, 207–10.

22 See McKillop 1949; Levine 1967, 427–51; Schonhorn 1968, 433f.

23 See Schonhorn 1980, 555.

24 See Williams 1974, 205–6.

25 See Jex-Blake and Sellers 1896, xvi–xxxvi; Isager 1991, 104.

26 Richter 1974, chapter 3.

27 Berenson 1953, 72.

28 Horace, *Sat.* 2.3.259ff. is based on Terence, *Eun.* 46–63.

29 See Rudd 1966, 86–118.

30 Dryden, ed. Ker (1900, 2.102).

31 For Pope's, and his predecessors' opinions of Shakespeare see Nichol Smith 1903.

32 For illustration of these and other points see Lounsbury 1906, 52ff.

33 In *The Comedy of Errors* much of 3.1 and 4.6 is relegated. As a result the page presents two plays – a decorous neo-classical drama running along a narrow band at the top, and a boisterous comedy occupying all the rest.

34 See Guerinot 1969, xxix ff.

35 See, e.g., *Epist.* 1.19.7; *AP.* 57; *Sat.* 1.10.48–9.

36 E.g., George II did not listen to recitations (362–3).

37 See line 124, and cf. Pope's letter to Lord Oxford, 3 March 1726 (Sherburn 1956, 2.370).

38 At The Devil (42) Ben Jonson presided over the Apollo Club. Hence the presence of the Muses. There is a piquant contrast with the ancient passages where a poet encountered the Muses on Helicon or Parnassus.

39 The Champion was an official who issued a ritual challenge to any opponents of the new monarch. Line 319 might be taken to imply that Cibber played the Champion, but the Twickenham editor's note indicates that in fact he played Wolsey; in which case we must imagine the Champion's armour being reflected on Wolsey's chest. (For this explanation I am indebted to Dr David Hopkins.)

40 The slogan was rejected as early as Alcuin (c. 735–804), who in a letter to Charlemagne (*Epist.* 127) asserted that 'the riotousness of the crowd is always very close to madness' (*tumultuositas uulgi semper insaniae proxima*).

41 See Rudd 1984.

42 The most likely case is 'Then Marble, soften'd into life, grew warm' (147), which recalls the stones of Deucalion and Pyrrha turning into people: *paulatimque anima caluerunt mollia saxa* (Juvenal 1.83) 'and gradually the stones grew warm and soft with life.'

43 Though conscious of Chaucer's grossness, Pope greatly admired his comic narrative. See Tillotson's Preface to vol. 2 of the Twickenham edition, especially 7–12.

   John Skelton (1460? – 1529) was made poet laureate at Oxford and Cambridge (and Louvain) – an academic rather than a royal honour; hence 'Heads of Houses quote.' Pope may have formed an initial opinion of Skelton on the basis of the low-life poem 'The Tunnyng of Elynour Rummyng,' which was reprinted in 1718. 'The effect,' says Auden, 'is like looking at the human skin through a magnifying glass' (Edwards 1981, 184). But if Pope had read the first item in the collected edition of 1568 (reprinted 1736), he would have seen that Skelton was capable of writing on quite another level.

44 Lines 156–60 are also political, unlike the original.

45 Pope is stretching a point here; for Swift's successes were not achieved by poetry.

46 According to Pope's Advertisement (22ff.), Horace claims that the introduction of the polite arts of Greece had improved the morals of Roman writers. In fact the restraint of slander, and the development of decent language (155) were due to the introduction of the Twelve Tables in the fifth century. The improvements attributed

to Greek influence are thought of, not as moral, but as stylistic, and even they are treated in very general terms.

47 Dobson 1913, 301–5.

Chapter Four

1 'Set sail in your bark and flee from every form of culture,' Epicurus, Frag. 33 (Bailey 1926). For information on Epicurus and Lucretius see Clay 1983, and his bibliography.

2 Lucretius was aware of the danger described by Rémy de Gourmont as follows: 'the ages of faith have heaped upon our minds such amassments of rhetoric and mystery, that now, when we seek natural explanations for lofty and beautiful things, we seem to commit a coarse triviality,' 366–7.

3 Hume 1935, 199–200. Cf. F.W. Newman's formulation: 'A God uncaused and existing from eternity is to the full as incomprehensible as a world uncaused and existing from eternity' (1849, 36). Tennyson was well aware of the point; see H. Tennyson 1897, 1.352.

4 'The finest description of sexual intercourse ever written was in Dryden's translation of Lucretius.' See Jeffares 1962, 267.

5 Munro's translation reads: 'Death to us is nothing, concerns us not a jot, since the nature of the mind is proved to be mortal; and as in time gone by we felt no distress, when the Poeni from all sides came together to do battle, and all things shaken by war's troublous uproar shuddered and quaked beneath high heaven, and mortal men were in doubt which of the two peoples it should be to whose empire all must fall by sea and land alike, thus when we shall be no more, when there shall have been a separation of body and soul, out of both of which we are each formed into a single being, to us, you may be sure, who then shall be no more, nothing whatever can happen to excite sensation, not if earth shall be mingled with sea, and sea with heaven' (*DRN* 3.830–41).

6 See Mayhew 1851, vol 1, e.g., 254–7, 412–14, 477–85, and Simon's reports printed in Pike 1967, 271ff. This, of course, was Dickens's London.

7 For a summary of Pengelly's work see the appendix to H. Pengelly 1897.

8 There is a delightful essay on Boucher de Perthes in Butler 1990, 159–69.

9 The date of completion, apparently, was Friday, 26 October 4004 BC.

10 Hennell 1838, 481. The new biblical criticism was expounded in Trinity College Cambridge by Connop Thirlwall and Julius Hare.

11 Hennell 1838, xiii.

12 Spencer, e.g., says, 'The will comes into existence through the increasing complexity and imperfect coherence of automatic actions' (1870, 498–9).

13 H. Tennyson 1897, 2.57.

14 Reade 1872, 430. A creator was accepted by Lyell, 'An Infinite and Eternal Being' (1914, 621); Chambers, 'Let no one suppose there is any necessary disrespect for the Creator in thus tracing his laws' (1884, 146); Darwin, 'There is a grandeur in this view of life ... having been originally breathed by the Creator into a few forms or into one' (1951, 560); Spencer, more vaguely, speaks of 'manifestations of the Unknowable,' 2.311.

15 C. Tennyson 1954, 76.

16 *To the Rev. F.D. Maurice*, Ricks no. 312, especially stanzas 2 and 3; cf. note 50 below.

17 H. Tennyson 1897, 1.320.

18 See Brown 1947, 18, 20, 26, 41, 243.

19 '[If I thought our hope of personal immortality was not true] I'd sink my head tonight in a chloroformed handkerchief and have done with it all,' quoted by Knowles 1893, 169. Cf. Martin 1980, 482; *In Memoriam* XXXIV; *Despair* VI; *Vastness*, headnote in Ricks and stanza XVII.

20 'It's too hopeful, this poem, more than I am myself,' quoted by Knowles 1893, 182.

21 *On the Jubilee of Queen Victoria*, Ricks no. 418, IX.

22 'It is no uncommon thing, in a room 12 feet square or less, to find three or four families *styed* together (perhaps with infectious disease among them), filling the same space night and day – men, women, and children in the promiscuous intimacy of cattle. Of these inmates it is nearly superfluous to observe that in all offices of nature they are gregarious and public; that every instinct of personal or sexual decency is stifled; that every nakedness of life is uncovered there,' Simon, in Pike 1967, 277. See further Wolkovitz 1991.

23 A.E. Housman, *Last Poems*, IX.25.

24 Martin 1980, 517, 556, 577. Graves speaks of Tennyson quoting unsavoury anecdotes from Brantôme, but condemning the immorality of the sensual world (1926, 344).

25 The topicality increased as a result of Tennyson's poem; see Turner 1973, 335ff.

26 'Had I been taught Greek and Latin I would now be a properly educated man, and would not have to look in useless longing at books that have been, through the poor mechanism of translation, the builders of my soul, nor face authority with the timidity born of excuse and evasion,' 58–9.

27 H. Tennyson 1897, 2.500; cf. C. Tennyson 1954, 188–97. Those who have heard the old cylinder recording of Tennyson reading *The Charge of the Light Brigade* will find corroboration in Knowles, who speaks of him as having 'a grand deep measured voice,' and as 'rather intoning on a few notes than speaking' (1893, 171). Parry remarked: 'He was given to a rather commonplace lilt – a sing-song method of enforcing the accents which rather jarred with my sense of the rhythmic variety of the written verse' (Graves 1926, 346–7). Parry records Tennyson's comment on Browning: 'It's strange; Browning was a musical man, and understood music, but there's no music in his verse. Now I am unmusical, and I don't understand music, but I know there's music in my verse. (ibid)' To recapture the effect of Tennyson reading Lucretius, one must also bear in mind that the poet will have used the traditional English pronunciation of Latin.

28 For the story, see Bailey 1947, 1.8–9.

29 See Wilkinson 1949, 47–8. Nepos is cited in Plutarch, *Lucullus* 43; cf. Pliny, *N.H.* xxv.25.

30 Lachmann 1853, 63: *Liuia uirum suum interfecit, quem nimis odiit; Lucillia suum, quem nimis amauit. illa sponte miscuit aconitum, haec decepta furorem propinauit pro amoris poculo* ... , 'Livia killed her husband out of excessive hatred, Lucillia hers out of excessive love. The former mixed poison deliberately, the latter unwittingly administered madness instead of a love potion.' This passage is to be found in Migne, *Patrologia Latina* 30, col. 259, section 23. It is not by Jerome, but is associated with him in the tradition. One notes that it does not identify Lucillia as Lucretius' wife. Cf. D.L. Chambers 1903.

31 Contrast the happiness described in *DRN* 3.894–6, where the husband's heart is 'touched with quiet joy' at the welcome he receives from his wife and children.

32 Euripides has: ἀλλ', ὡς ἐσεῖδες μαστόν, ἐκβαλών ξίφος φίλημ' ἐδέξω (*Andromache* 628–9). The scene appears on Greek vases; see, e.g., Boardman 1975, fig. 158; 1989, fig. 309.

33 Cf. 4.1058, where 'Venus' is the name given to sexual desire.

34 The sun took vengeance on the Greeks for slaughtering his oxen.

See *Odyssey* 12.374–96. Tennyson found the name Hyperion ('the one passing overhead') in line 374 of that passage.

35 *The Lotos-Eaters*, Ricks no. 170.155.

36 According to Epicurus, the breast was the seat of the emotions: 'for here throb fear and apprehension; about these spots dwell soothing joys' (*DRN* 3.140–2).

37 When Keats's *Ode on a Grecian Urn* is recited in polite schools, it is perhaps not always realized that this is what the poet had in mind by 'What maidens loth? / What mad pursuit? What struggle to escape?'

38 Cleopatra was determined not to be dragged in arrogant triumph – *deduci superbo triumpho* (Horace, *Odes* 1.37.31–2).

39 Lines 249ff. 'But till this cosmic order everywhere / ... Cracks all to pieces' etc. The words 'cosmic order,' however, tend to be misleading. When Lucretius speaks of the *moles et machina mundi* falling apart (5.96), that means, as Munro renders it, 'the mass and fabric of the world,' not 'of the universe,' as in the translation in Ricks's note.

40 Nepos, *Life of Atticus*, 22. (Nepos is printed with Florus in the Loeb edition.)

41 With the possible exception of the small point noted in note 39 above, this appears to be the only inaccuracy in Tennyson's description of Epicureanism. Tranquillity (*ataraxia*) was not 'without one pleasure.' On the contrary, it represented the finest kind of pleasure. Certainly it should not be equated with the lack of feeling.

42 See Bailey 1947, 1.17–18 and 1940, 284ff.

43 One sometimes forgets that since Lucretius' atoms are invisible, the descriptions of their behaviour are necessarily imaginative as well as scientific. This does not mean, however, that the *DRN* is uniformly poetic, as some recent critics would have us believe.

44 See Kozicki 1979, 157ff.

45 In the description of the much-edited Oread 'And here an Oread – how the sun delights / To glance and shift about her slippery sides' (188–9) one wonders whether 'sides' would have carried any erotic charge to the reader. The Latin *latus*, apparently, was capable of doing so; see Ovid, *Amores* 1.5.22 (*quantum et quale latus*) and Horace, *Satires* 1.2.93. I take 'slippery,' like *lubricus*, to mean 'hard to grasp,' 'sinuous,' 'wriggling.'

46 Kozicki (1979, 158–9) is right to oppose both Bush's statement that '[Lucretius'] creed has failed him' and the inference drawn by John-

son that 'the unaided reason is not in itself strong and sure enough to discipline man's sensual nature.' Lucretius, after all, had been poisoned. The same point tells against Buckley's contention (1967, 168) that '[Tennyson's] concern was to demonstrate the inadequacy of even the highest naturalistic philosophy to provide an incentive for either the humane life or the arts that embody humanity's aspiration.' There is worthwhile material in Marion Shaw's study, but she goes much too far in characterizing Tennyson as 'a misogynist poet to whom women, if not in life then at least in the imaginative scheme his poetry offers, represent fear and loathing and, even more invidious, self-loathing' (1988, 141).

47 Ixion and his wheel are not in Lucretius' text. They are, however, in the words supplied by Munro to fill a gap, on the basis of a note in Servius.

48 See, e.g., Ovid *Met.* 10.40–7, which mentions Ixion and the Eumenides (Furies) among others.

49 In 1892 Tennyson confided to a bishop that he did not believe in hell. The bishop replied in a whisper that he didn't either (Graves 1926, 346).

50 Rudd 1991, 12.

Chapter 5

1 Tullus' uncle, L. Volcacius Tullus, a supporter of Augustus, was pro-consul of Asia Minor in 29–28 BC.

2 Callimachus, *Aetia* 1.21–8 (Loeb ed. p. 6).

3 Giving Pound the benefit of the doubt, one assumes that Pelion was intended to be on top of Ossa, and that the causeway would lead to heaven.

4 If DuQuesnay (1992, 78–83) is right, as I think he is, about 1.21 and 1.22, there are signs that Propertius was accepting Augustus before the publication of Book 1 (c.29 BC).

5 *Ore rotundo,* in Horace, *AP* 323, does not mean 'grand and resonant,' but 'easily flowing.'

6 In 2.16, Antony is held responsible for Actium; the ensuing peace has been due to Augustus. In 3.11, Propertius, dominated by Cynthia, recalls other masterful women, the most striking being Cleopatra who threatened to rule Rome as a foreign queen. There are divergent views of the quality of the 'Callimachean' hymn in honour of Actium (4.6); but it can hardly be seen as anything but a serious poem. See Sweet (1972), and more recently, Cairns (1984).

Pound did not use any of these elegies. Nor did he use 2.7. This, the one overtly rebellious poem, asserts that Propertius will never father a soldier (14). The tone comes from the fact that a law (recently withdrawn) had threatened the poet's all-important relationship with Cynthia. For a full discussion of these tensions in Propertius, see Stahl 1985.

7 In 4.3, 'Arethusa' writes movingly to 'Lycotas,' who is away on active service; despite their names, the two characters are not only Romans but also wife and husband. In 4.4, it is told how a young woman in love betrays her city to the enemy, like Scylla in Ovid, *Met.* 8.84–100. But again the young woman is Roman; Tarpeia's action explains the name of the rock. The epyllion of Hercules and Cacus in *Aen.* 8 is recalled in 4.9; but, like 4.4, it is an aetiological poem, explaining the absence of women from the ceremony of the *Ara Maxima*. In 4.11, the aristocratic Cornelia addresses her husband from the grave. The poem is an expression of love, but it is the married love of a Roman matron. It is doubtful if Pound read Book 4 with any care. He does not draw on it in *Homage*, except perhaps indirectly in the case of 4.8; and even 4.8 is called 'The Ride to Lanuvium,' a title which is far from apposite.

8 'Protection' for *tueri* is one of Pound's near misses. One suspects the mistake was unintentional, but certainty is impossible.

9 In 1922, Pound spoke of Propertius, 'tying blue ribbon in the tails of Virgil and Horace' (Paige 1951, 246).

10 The interestingly bi-focal quality of Propertius' poem is missing from Goethe's sentimental imitation, *Der Besuch*.

11 The allusion is to 4.7, especially 55–70. In *The Classics*, Johnson speaks of 'Propertius' ardent graces.'

12 The collection called *Decorations* once had an epigraph taken from Propertius 1.11.23ff.

13 W.Y. Sellar (1892) and H.E. Butler (1905) both saw Propertius as solemn and gloomy; but S.G. Tremenheere, on p.xii of his elegant verse translation (1899), referred to his wide range of feeling and his genial humour. Classical scholars seldom speak with one voice. It is interesting to note that in the last few years it has once again become possible to discuss the romantic element in Propertius (see Papanghelis 1987). 'Thus the whirligig of time brings in his revenges.'

14 In spite of its faintly sarcastic tone, the phrase recalls Girodet's painting *Endymion*, in which Diana's moonbeams fall brightly on the flesh of the sleeping shepherd. For illustration see Honour 1968, Plate 79.

15 In line 53, Pound, following Müller's text, translates *spiramus*. Apparently as the result of a slip, Sullivan prints the manuscript's uncorrected reading, *speramus*.

16 'The sexless American professor' is a stereotype with which I am not familiar.

17 In *How to Read* (1927–8), reprinted in Eliot 1960, 15–40; *logopoeia* is described on p. 25.

18 The procedure is followed to eccentric lengths in Zukovsky's 'translation' of Catullus.

19 The dedication of *A Lume Spento* (1908) reads *in memoriam eius mihi caritate primus* William Brooke Smith. Other examples include *In tempore senectus* (see King 1976, 298); *Lucifer Caditurus; Fragmenti;* and *Blandula, Tenulla, Vagula.* In the last case it is not enough to say that *tenulla* is just a misprint for *tenella;* the word is not in the original at all. Hadrian's line reads *animula, uagula, blandula* (Morel 1963, 137).

20 In the *Literary Essays* we have such examples as *uir quidem* (Eliot 1960, 71); *penitus enim tibi O Phoebe attributa est cantus* (91); *ingenium nobis ipsa puella fecit* (145, 151, 343) – an interesting case in view of Pound's much-praised sensitivity to cadence; *pars labitinam uitabit* (369); *in saeculum saeculorum* (407). In the *Letters* we have Greek as well as Latin examples: *ueritas pareualebit* (Paige 1951, 54); *Delphos* (68); *kenos issos* (116); *opusculus* (146); *condit* (founded) (285); *neson amumona,* literally the narrow island (285).

21 Pound's strictures were not, of course, confined to the classics. Tolstoy, e.g., was a Russian, 'therefore a mess' (Carpenter 1988, 43). Wordsworth was 'a dull sheep'; Byron's technique was 'rotten.' His accolades could be just as embarrassing. Golding's *Metamorphoses* was 'possibly the most beautiful book in our language'; Gavin Douglas's *Aeneid* was better than the original; Landor was 'perhaps the only complete and serious man of letters ever born in these islands.'

22 See *OLD, uerto* 24a.

Appendix

1 According to C.D. Buck (1928, 226), 'he had a keen appreciation of, and fine taste in, all forms of art.'

2 See the asterisked items in Enk 1948, 78–83.

3 Many modern editors read *ut solito,* which removes the confusion.

4 Pound's subsequent protest (Paige 1951, 212) is both disingenuous

and unnecessary: 'Precisely what I do not do is to translate the *in* as if it negatived the *solito*.'

5 Kenner is one of Pound's most eloquent and ingenious advocates. One can accept his excellent description of Pound's method as 'the deliberate *collage* of poker-faced misreadings' (1951, 151). But it is the purpose and effect of such misreadings that cause problems. Addressing Virgil, Propertius says: '*tale facis carmen docta testudine quale / Cynthius impositis temperat articulis*' (2.34.79–80). Kenner translates: 'Such music makest thou as the Cynthian god [Apollo] modulates with fingers pressed upon his well-skilled lyre.' He then quotes Pound's farcically garbled version: 'Like a trained and performing tortoise, / I would make verse in your fashion, if she should command it, / With her husband asking a remission of sentence' (Section XII). Very well, let us give up any hope of coherence. (To whom does Pound think he is talking?) We can see that 'tortoise' comes from *testudine*. And with a stretch of the imagination we can see that the pentameter has been used twice: (a) Cynthia imposes commands, (b) her husband (Cynthius) modifies terms imposed. But when we have worked out all this verbal horse-play, we may still think it a bit extravagant when Kenner praises the first two lines as a 'superbly impressionistic distich.'

6 For a more specific account see Rudd 1972, vii–xvii.

7 He suffered digestive troubles and insomnia for the rest of his life. See Hayman, 1976, ch. 1.

8 Conversely, writers about Propertius, e.g., Benediktson (1989), show a positive interest in Pound. This trend began with Sullivan's book on Propertius (1976).

Bibliography

The following works are referred to in the text and notes.

Chapter One

Ames, R.M. 1986. 'The Feminist Connections of Chaucer's *Legend of Good Women*.' In *Chaucer in the Eighties*, edd. J.N. Wasserman and R.J. Blanch. Syracuse, 57–7

Anderson, W.S. 1973. 'The *Heroides*.' In *Ovid*, ed. J.W. Binns. London and Boston, 49–8

Austin, R.G. 1964. *P. Vergili Maronis Aeneidos Liber Secundus*. Oxford

– 1971 *P. Vergili Maronis Aeneidos Liber Primus*. Oxford

Bennett, J.A.W. 1968. *Chaucer's Book of Fame*. Oxford

Benson, L.D. 1986. 'The "Love-Tydinges" in Chaucer's *House of Fame*'. In *Chaucer in the Eighties*, edd. J.N. Wasserman and R.J. Blanch. Syracuse, 3–22

Boitani, P., ed. 1983. *Chaucer and the Italian Trecento*. Cambridge

– 1984. *Chaucer and the Imaginary World of Fame*. Cambridge

Brewer, D.S., ed. 1978. *Chaucer: The Critical Heritage, 1385–1935*, Vol. 1. London

Burck, E. 1943. 'Das Bild der Karthager in der römischen Literatur.' In *Rom und Karthago*, ed. J. Vogt. Leipzig, 336–45

Burrow, J.A. 1991. 'Poems without Endings.' *Studies in the Age of Chaucer* 13, 17–37

Clemen, W. 1980. *Chaucer's Early Poetry*, Eng. trans. London and New York, repr.

Cooper, H. 1988. 'Chaucer and Ovid: A Question of Authority.' In *Ovid Renewed*, ed. C.A. Martindale. Cambridge, 71–81

Delany, S. 1972. *Chaucer's House of Fame*. Chicago and London

Evans, J. 1930. 'Chaucer and Decorative Art.' *RES* 6, 408–12

Fyler, J.M. 1979. *Chaucer and Ovid*. New Haven and London

Harbert, B. 1974. 'Chaucer and the Latin Classics.' In *Geoffrey Chaucer*, ed. D.S. Brewer. London, 137–53

Hopkins, D.W.1988. 'Dryden and Ovid's "Wit out of Season." ' In *Ovid Renewed*, ed. C.A. Martindale. Cambridge, 167–90

Horsfall, N. 1990. 'Dido in the Light of History.' Repr. in *Oxford Readings in Vergil's Aeneid*, ed. S.J. Harrison. Oxford, 127–44

Jacobson, H. 1974. *Ovid's Heroides*. Princeton

Kiser, L.J. 1983. *Telling Classical Tales: Chaucer and the Legend of Good Women*. Ithaca

Kittredge, G.L. 1963 [1915]. *Chaucer and his Poetry*. Cambridge, MA

Mann, J. 1991. *Geoffrey Chaucer*. London

Martin, P. 1990. *Chaucer's Women*. London

Minnis, A.J. 1986. 'From Medieval to Renaissance: Chaucer's Position on Past Gentility,' *Proc. British Academy* 72, 205–46

– 1991. '*De Vulgari Auctoritate*: Chaucer, Gower and the Men of Great Authority.' In *Chaucer and Gower: Difference, Mutuality, Exchange*, ed. R.F. Yeager. *Eng. Lit. Stud.* 36, University of Victoria, 36–74

Muscadine, C. 1957. *Chaucer and the French Tradition*. Berkeley

Otis, B. 1964. *Virgil: A Study in Civilised Poetry*. Oxford

Pease, A.S. 1967. *Publi Vergili Maronis Aeneidos Liber Quartus*. Repr. Darmstadt

Prescott, H.W. 1963 [1927]. *The Development of Vergil's Art*. Chicago.

Quinn, K. 1968. *Virgil's Aeneid: A Critical Description*. London.

Rudd, N. 1976. 'Dido's *Culpa*.' In *Lines of Enquiry*. Cambridge; repr. in *Oxford Readings in Vergil's Aeneid*, ed. S.J. Harrison. Oxford 1990, 145–66

Shannon, E.F. 1964. *Chaucer and the Roman Poets*. Repr. New York

Shook, L.K. 1968. 'The House of Fame.' In *Companion to Chaucer Studies*, ed. B. Rowland. Oxford, 341–54

Spearing, A.C. 1976. *Medieval Dream Poetry*. Cambridge

Steadman, J.M. 1961. 'Chaucer's Desert of Lybye, Venus and Jove.' *MLN* 76, 196–201

Verducci, F. 1985. *Ovid's Toyshop of the Heart*. Princeton

Wallace, D. 1985. *Chaucer and the Early Writings of Boccaccio*. Woodbridge

Wilkinson, L.P. 1955. *Ovid Recalled*. Cambridge

Wimsatt, J.I. 1974. 'Chaucer and French Poetry.' In *Geoffrey Chaucer*, ed. D.S. Brewer. London, 109–36

Windeatt, B.A. 1982. *Chaucer's Dream Poetry*. Cambridge
Winsor (Leach), E.J. 1963. 'A Study in the Sources and Rhetoric of Chaucer's *Legend of Good Women* and Ovid's *Heroides*.' Diss. Yale
Wrenn, C.L. 1923. 'Chaucer's Knowledge of Horace,' *MLR* 18, 286–92

Chapter Two

Baldwin, T.W. 1944. *William Shakespeare's Small Latin and Less Greek*, 2 vols. Urbana
– 1965. *On the Compositional Genetics of the Comedy of Errors*. Urbana
Bullough, G. 1957. *Narrative and Dramatic Sources of Shakespeare*, vol. 1. London
Edmonds, J.M. 1959 and 1961. *The Fragments of Attic Comedy*, vols. 2 and 3. Leiden
Foakes, R.A. 1962. *The Comedy of Errors*. London
Frye, N. 1957. *Anatomy of Criticism*. Princeton and London
Gesner, C. 1970. *Shakespeare and the Greek Romance*. Lexington
Goolden, P. 1958. *The Old English Apollonius of Tyre*. Oxford
Greenblatt, S. 1988. *Shakespearean Negotiations*. Oxford
O'Brien-Moore, A. 1924. *Madness in Ancient Literature*. Princeton
Perry, B.E. 1967. *The Ancient Romances*. Berkeley and Los Angeles
Quiller-Couch, A., and J. Dover Wilson. 1962. *The Comedy of Errors*, 2d ed. Cambridge
Reardon, B.P. 1989. *Collected Ancient Greek Novels*. London
Rudd, N. 1979. 'Pyramus and Thisbe in Shakespeare and Ovid.' In *Creative Imitation and Latin Literature*, edd. D. West and T. Woodman. Cambridge, 173–93
Salingar, L. 1974. *Shakespeare and the Traditions of Comedy*. Cambridge.
Segal, E. 1969. *Plautus: Three Comedies*. New York/London
Turner, P. 1957. *The Ephesian Story*. London

Chapter Three

Berenson, B. 1953. *Italian Painting of the Renaissance*. London
Bloom, L. 1964. 'Pope as a Textual Critic' in *Essential Articles for the Study of Alexander Pope*, ed. M. Mack. London, 495–506
Brink, C.O. 1982. *Horace on Poetry*, vol. 3. Cambridge
Butt, J. 1936. *Pope's Taste in Shakespeare*. London
Dobson, A. 1913. *Collected Poems*. London
Edwards, A.S.G., ed. 1981. *Skelton, the Critical Heritage*. London

Erskine-Hill, H. 1983. *The Augustan Idea in English Literature*. London

Fishwick, D. 1987. *The Imperial Cult in the Latin West*, vol. 1 (in two parts). Leiden.

Fraenkel, E. 1957. *Horace*. Oxford

Fuchs, J. 1989. *Reading Pope's Imitations of Horace*

Goldstein, W. 1958. *Pope and the Augustan Stage*. Stanford

Grierson, H.J.C., ed. 1980 [1912]. *The Poems of John Donne*, 2 vols. Oxford

Guerinot, J.V. 1969. *Pamphlet Attacks on Alexander Pope, 1711–1744*. London

Isager, J. 1991. *Pliny on Art and Society*. London and New York

Jex-Blake, K., and E. Sellers. 1896. *The Elder Pliny's Chapters on the History of Art*. London

Jones, A.H.M. 1977. *Augustus*. London

Ker, W.P. 1900. *Essays of John Dryden*, 2 vols. Oxford

Levine, J.A. 1967. 'Pope's Epistle to Augustus, 1–30.' *Studies in English Literature*, 7, 427–51

Lounsbury, T.R. 1906. *The First Editions of Shakespeare*. London

Mack, M. 1969. *The Garden and the City*. Toronto and London

McKillop, A.D. 1949. 'Ethics and Political History in Thomson's *Liberty*.' In *Pope and His Contemporaries*, edd. J.L. Clifford and L.A. Landa. Oxford, 215–29

Nichol Smith, D. 1903. *Eighteenth Century Essays on Shakespeare*. Glasgow

Price, S.R.F. 1986. *Rituals and Power*. Cambridge

Rice-Holmes, T. 1928 and 1931. *The Architect of the Roman Empire*, 2 vols. Oxford

Richter, G. 1974. *A Handbook of Greek Art*, 7th ed. London and New York

Rudd, N. 1966. *The Satires of Horace*. Cambridge

– 1984. 'Pope and Horace on Not Writing Poetry.' In *English Satire and the Satiric Tradition*, ed. C. Rawson. Oxford, 167–82

Schonhorn, M. 1968. 'The Audacious Contemporaneity of Pope's *Epistle to Augustus*.' *Studies in English Literature* 8, 431–43

–1980. 'Pope's *Epistle to Augustus*: Notes Towards a Mythology.' In *Pope: Recent Essays*, edd. M. Mack and J. Winn. Brighton, 546–64

Sherburn, G. 1956. *The Correspondence of Alexander Pope*, 5 vols. Oxford

Spence, J. 1966. *Observations, Anecdotes and Characters of Books and Men*, ed. J.M. Osborn, 2 vols. Oxford

Stack, F. 1985. *Pope and Horace*. Cambridge

Syme, R. 1939. *The Roman Revolution*. Oxford

Taylor, L.R. 1931. *The Divinity of the Roman Emperor*. Middleton, CT

Warburton, W. 1752. *The Works of Alexander Pope*, vol. 4. London

Warton, J. 1756/82. *Essay on the Genius and Writings of Pope*. London

– 1797. *The Works of Alexander Pope*, vol. 4. London

Weinbrot, H.D. 1978. *Augustus Caesar in 'Augustan' England*. Princeton

Williams, B. 1974. *The Whig Supremacy*, 2d ed. Oxford

Zanker, P. and K. Vierneisel. 1979. *Die Bildnisse des Augustus*. München

Zanker, P. 1990. *The Power of Images in the Age of Augustus*, Eng. trans. Ann Arbor

Chapter Four

Bailey, C. 1926. 1. *Epicurus*. Oxford

– 1940. 'The Mind of Lucretius.' *AJP* 61, 278–91

– 1947. *Titi Lucreti Cari de Rerum Natura Libri Sex*, 3 vols. Oxford

Bain, A. 1894. *The Senses and the Intellect*, 4th ed. London

Boardman, J. 1975. *Athenian Red Figure Vases: The Archaic Period*. London

– 1989. *Athenian Red Figure Vases: The Classical Period*. London

Brown, A.W. 1947. *The Metaphysical Society: Victorian Minds in Crisis, 1869–1880*. New York

Buckley, J.H. 1967. *Tennyson: The Growth of a Poet*. Cambridge, MA

Bury, J.B. 1920. *The Idea of Progress*. London

Butler, H. 1990. *The Sub-Prefect Should Have Held His Tongue and Other Essays*. London

Chambers, D.L. 1903. 'Tennysoniana.' *MLN* 18, 231–2

Chambers, R. 1884 [1844], *Vestiges of the Natural History of Creation*, 8th ed. London and Edinburgh

Clay, D. 1983. *Lucretius and Epicurus*. Ithaca and London

Colenso, J.W. 1862–79. *The Pentateuch and the Book of Joshua Critically Examined*. London

Darwin, C. 1951 [1859]. *The Origin of Species*, 6th ed. repr. London

Gerhard, J. 1968. *Tennysonian Love: The Strange Diagonal*. Minneapolis

Gourmont, R. de. 1984 [1953]. *Poudre aux Moineaux*, trans. E. Pound, *Translations*. London, 361–97

Graves, C.L. 1926. *Hubert Parry*, vol. 1. London

Hennell, C.C. 1838. *An Enquiry Concerning the Origin of Christianity*. London

Hume, D. 1935. *Dialogues on Natural Religion*, ed. N. Kemp Smith. Oxford

Jeffares, A.N. 1962. *W.B. Yeats – Man and Mask*, 2d ed. London

Knowles, J.1893. 'Aspects of Tennyson II.' *Nineteenth Century* 33, 164–88

Kozicki, H. 1979. *Tennyson and Clio*. Baltimore and London

Lachmann, C. 1853. *T. Lucreti Cari De Rerum Natura Libri Sex*. Berlin

Lecky, W.E.H. 1865. *History of the Rise and Influence of the Spirit of Rationalism in Europe*, 2d ed., 2 vols. London

Lyell, C.1875. *Principles of Geology*, 12th ed., 2 vols. London

– 1914. *The Geological Evidence of the Antiquity of Man*. London

Martin, R.B. 1980. *Tennyson: The Unquiet Heart*. Oxford

Mayhew, H. 1851. *London Labour and the London Poor*, 2 vols. London

Munro, H.A.J. 1898 and 1900. *T. Lucreti Cari De Rerum Natura Libri Sex*, 4th ed., 3 vols. London

Newman, F.W. 1849. *The Soul, Her Sorrows and Her Aspirations*. London

Pengelly, H.1897. *A Memoir of William Pengelly*. London

Pike, E.R. 1967. *Human Documents of the Victorian Golden Age*. London

Reade, Winwood. 1872. *The Martyrdom of Man*. London

Renan, E. 1863. *The Life of Jesus*, Eng. trans. London

Ricks, C.B. 1987. *The Poems of Tennyson*, 2d ed., 3 vols. London

Rudd, N. 1991. 'Two Invitations: Tennyson, *To the Rev. F.D. Maurice*, and Horace, *Odes* 3.29.' *Hermathena* 150, 5–19

Shaw, M. 1988. *Alfred Lord Tennyson*. London

Spencer, H.1870. *Principles of Psychology*, 2 vols., 2d ed. London

Strauss, D.F. 1848. *The Life of Jesus*, Eng. trans. London

Tennyson, C. 1954. *Six Tennyson Essays*. London

Tennyson, H. 1897. *Tennyson: A Memoir*, 2 vols. London

Turner, F.M. 1973. 'Lucretius among the Victorians.' *Victorian Studies* 16, 329–48

Wilkinson, L.P. 1949. 'Lucretius and the Love Potion.' *CR*, 63, 47–8

Wolkovitz, J.R. 1991. *The City of Dreadful Delight*. Chicago

Yeats, W.B. 1961. *Autobiographies*, repr. London

Chapter Five and Appendix

Arkins, B. 1988. 'Pound's Propertius: What Kind of Homage?' *Paideuma* 17, 29–44

Benediktson, T.D. 1989. *Propertius: Modernist Poet of Antiquity*. Carbondale Edwardsville

Buck, C.D. 1928. 'William Gardner Hale.' *University Records* 14.4, Chicago, 225–6

Butler, H.E. 1905. *Sexti Properti Opera Omnia*. London

Cairns, F. 1984. 'Propertius and the Battle of Actium.' In *Poetry and Politics in the Age of Augustus*, edd. T. Woodman and D. West, Cambridge. 129–68

Carpenter, H. 1988. *A Serious Character: The Life of Ezra Pound*. London

Conquest, R. 1963. 'Ezra Pound.' *London Magazine* 3.1, 33–49

Cookson, W. 1973. *Ezra Pound: Selected Prose 1909–1965*.

Davie, D. 1991. *Studies in Ezra Pound*. Manchester

Dowson, E. 1934. *The Poetical Works*, ed. D. Flower. London

DuQuesnay, I.M. le M. 1992. 'In Memoriam Galli.' In *Author and Audience in Latin Literature*, edd. T. Woodman and J. Powell. Cambridge, 52–83

Edwards, M.W. 1961. 'Intensification of Meaning in Propertius and Others.' *TAPA* 92, 128–44

Eliot, T.S. 1948 [1928]. *Ezra Pound: Selected Poems*. London

– 1960 [1954]. *Literary Essays of Ezra Pound*. London

Enk, P.J. 1946. *Sex. Propertii Elegiarum Liber 1*, Pars Prior. Leiden

Flach, D. 1967. *Das literarische Verhältnis von Horaz und Properz*. Giessen

Gantillon, P.J.F. 1878. *Propertius*. Bohn Library, London

Goodwin, K.L. 1966. *The Influence of Ezra Pound*. London

Goold, G.P. 1990. *Propertius*. Loeb Classical Library, Cambridge, MA, and London

Graves, R. 1955. 'Dr. Syntax and Mr. Pound.' In *The Crowning Privilege*. London, 212–14

Hayman, R. 1976. *Leavis*. London

Hendrickson, G.L. 1928. 'William Gardner Hale.' *CJ* 24, 167–73

Homberger, E. 1972. *Ezra Pound: The Critical Heritage*. London and Boston

Honour, H. 1968. *Neoclassicism*. Harmondsworth

Hooley, D.M. 1988. *The Classics in Paraphrase*. London and Toronto

Hubbard, M. 1974. *Propertius*. London

Johnson, L.P. 1915. *Poetical Works*, with preface by Ezra Pound. London

Kenner, H. 1951. *The Poetry of Ezra Pound*. London

King, M.J. 1976 [1926]. *Collected Early Poems of Ezra Pound*. London

Leavis, F.R. 1948. *Education and the University*. New York

MacKail, J.W. 1895. *Latin Literature*. New York

Messing, G.M. 1975. 'Pound's Propertius: The Homage and the Damage.' In *Poetry and Poetics from Ancient Greece to the Renaissance*, ed. G.M. Kirkwood. Ithaca and London, 105–33

Morel, W. 1963. *Fragmenta Poetarum Latinorum*, repr. Stuttgart

Paige, D.D. 1951. *The Letters of Ezra Pound, 1907–1941*. London

Papanghelis, T.D. 1987. *Propertius: A Hellenistic Poet on Love and Death*. Cambridge

Postgate, J.P. 1881. *Select Elegies of Propertius*. London

Richardson, L.J. 1947. 'Ezra Pound's Homage to Propertius.' *Yale Poetry Review* 6, 21–9

Rudd, N., ed. 1972. *Essays on Classical Literature*. Cambridge

Sellar, W.Y. 1892. *The Roman Poets of the Augustan Age: Horace and the Elegiac Poets*. Oxford

Stahl, H.P. 1985. *Propertius: 'Love' and 'War.'* Berkeley and London

Stock, N. 1970. *The Life of Ezra Pound*. London

Sullivan, J.P. 1964. *Ezra Pound and Sextus Propertius*. London

– 1976. *Propertius*. Cambridge

Sweet, F. 1972. 'Propertius and Political Panegyric.' *Arethusa* 5, 169–75

Thomas, R.E. 1983. *The Latin Masks of Ezra Pound*. Ann Arbor

Townend, G.B. 1961. 'Propertius among the Poets.' *G & R* 8, 36–49

Tremenheere, S.G. 1899. *The Cynthia of Propertius*. London

Tränkle, H. 1960. *Die Sprachkunst des Properz und die Tradition der lateinischen Dichtersprache*. Wiesbaden